To: Franchez, love ya!

Coven
Aqusalah   Enjoy our journey
Salaa
                            Peace

i

... Done All The Time

G. Aqueelah Salaam
Qa'id J. Salaam © 2020

Disclaimer:
The author has tried to recreate events, locales and
conversations from her memories of them. In order to
maintain their anonymity in some instances she has
changed the names of individuals and places.
The transcripts presented in this book are copied
verbatim from the actual court proceedings involving
Mr. Qa'id Salaam. With the exception of Mr. Salaam
and Mr. David Singleton of the Beyond Guilt Program,
names of all involved have been changed to protect
identity.

ISBN: **978-0-578-79095-4**

Editing and Formatted by: *April R. Wilson*
and Yusuf A. H. Salaam
Proof Reading by: *Janice AbuBakr*
Cover Design by: *Philip Duvall*

Contents

REVIEWS

What an honor to write a word of endorsement and encouragement to my sister, Gwen Aqueelah Salaam, as she becomes a first-time author. I view myself as one of her many sounding boards that helped her bring this project to life.

... *DONE ALL THE TIME*, was written in my opinion, so that she could birth out of her heart and soul all the many experiences and challenges she, her son Qa'id and other family members lived through during his unjust but necessary time of incarceration. Because Gwen is a teacher and mentor at heart, I believe she also wanted to share with other families the lessons learned through disappointment and the sense of failure they all suffered as they looked to so called professionals to rescue them from what seemed to be hell on earth.

As you read through the pages of ... *DONE ALL THE TIME,* you will be struck by the bias and double standards conjured up by the judicial system that was set up to bring a resolution and ending that would uphold their predetermined charges regardless of the lack of evidence and or witnesses.

I believe with all my heart that GOD used Gwen and Qa'id to show the depth of His Love and the unwavering Faith she possesses that eventually opened the doors to the freedom that only He can give.

Your sister,
Barbara Moore

As history has clearly shown us there is no substitute for a mother's love for her child. Couple that with great faith in God and you have an example of resilience unparalleled. This is the story of that faith, that love, and that resilience.

Thank God for a mother's love and thank God for mothers like Aqueelah Salaam and this book. It is simply a love story of the most important kind.

CONGRATULATIONS!!!!!
Janice AbuBakr

... Done All The Time is a heartbreaking real talk application of a mother's personal real-life story of how she and her son endured the ups and downs of an unfair judicial system.

... Done All The Time entails a captivating story of a series of events that is written with heartfelt love, compassion, conviction and truth. Mrs. Salaam creates the backdrop from her son's birth, all the joys, the heartache and growing pains of raising a child, right down to the transformational processes of change. Seeing her son go from an angry teenaged boy to a responsible man from within the prison walls all within a span of 13 years, Mrs. Salaam endured visitations, prison phone calls, food and clothes boxes and even the deviating feeling of the disconnect of unfairly losing a child to the system. She tells her chilly story of crooked lawyers bending judicial system rules, and of a hope that never died.

This book not only exposes the wickedness of some of the untold truths behind prison walls, but it also highlights the hope of true transformation and unity. Written with a heart to see others survive, this book is a must-read for all those who are still waiting, those who are still hoping, and for those who believe in lasting change. This is an easy read and should be a gift to any family for a beacon of hope!

Mrs. Stacie L Johnson M.A, CDCA Ed. D
Candidate Intervention Specialist

... _DONE ALL THE TIME_ is an eye-opener to the "legal" injustices that go on behind closed doors. Quid Pro Quo is a legal way to extort what the system hopes to gain by offering plea deals that, at times, fail to benefit everyone involved *except* the legal system.

In her first book, Mrs. Salaam is unafraid to tell the truth and expose the lies, the half-truths and broken promises behind the judicial Quid Pro Quo.

Her story is a tale of Sacrifice and Suffering; Commitment and Dedication; Love and Faith.

... _DONE ALL THE TIME_ is a good read and I recommend it to anyone who has a loved one doing time.

Mrs. AW Jones

Preface

" There were times when my heart would sink when I was with my son. One day I happened to run into him on the street, so I picked him up. He was so much fun to be around, always smiling. We were talking and laughing about something when I slapped his leg. The laughter instantly stopped, replaced by nervousness when I felt a big gun! I hit a gun!

Instinct made me quickly pull over to the curb. I said, "You and your gun can get out!" I didn't care where he went either. I felt Satan was after me, but Satan was chasing him, and I was not going to get caught with him."

Two quotes:

"If people refuse to look at you in a new light and they can only see you for what you were, only see you for the mistakes you've made, if they don't realize that you are not your mistakes, then they have to be blocked out of your life, if only mentally" ...

"Never get on the wrong side of small-minded people with authority"! G. Aqueelah Salaam

Foreword

... *D̶o̶n̶e̶ A̶l̶l̶ T̶h̶e̶ T̶i̶m̶e̶* is a chronological exposé of a family tragedy. An event imposed on us and mainly suffered by my wife and youngest son (5th child of five children). Not a day or night went by without praying for our son in the jaws of the justice system. This young man's <u>MOTHER</u> is, and always has been, relentless in the pursuit of his release (MAMA BEAR). The day-to-day events, the phone calls, the monitoring of his Facebook page messages for him, the lawyers who dropped by the wayside, the letters written and the promises unkept over the thirteen years he was away made his siblings suffer with him as we all did the best we could until the day…Until *that* day.

That Day finally arrived. We heard good news and we knew he would soon be with us again. He has grown and learned so much that Allah has blessed him with another chance, a new mindset, a new spirit, a sense of self-worth, and, as he puts it, a new *"Thinking for a Change."*

His <u>MOTHER's cry,</u> "I hadn't finished raising him yet," resonates as she describes how he was swept away from before our eyes, and, *"We do this all the time"* became our reality. More than anything, we tried to ease her pain and support her every move, attempt, and strategy to secure justice from the jaws of a peculiar and particular institution that manifested its unwarranted position upon us. Yusuf A. H. Salaam

Words of Prophet Muhammad (PBUH)

And the Prophet would say:

Oh Allah,
Illuminate my Heart with Light and my Eyes
with Light and my Ears with Light.
Let there be Light on my Right and Light on
my Left.
Let there be Light Above me and Light
Below me.
Let there be Light in Front of me and Light
Behind me.

Oh Allah, Make me a Light.

May Allah's mercy make Qa'id a Light.
***As Salaam Alaikum*, (Peace Be Unto You)**

Acknowledgements

To those of you who visited Qa'id or loved him from a far …

To family and friends who tried to help guide us as a family with names of advocates or you blessed us with money, wrote letters of support and maybe you just listened or asked how Qa'id was doing….

WE THANK YOU FROM THE BOTTOM OF OUR ♥ HEARTS.

We give a Special Shout-Out to all who PRAYED for us.
God answered our PRAYERS!

Holy Qur'an Al-Hashr

(1)

Whatever is in the

Heavens and on Earth let

it declare the Praises are

Glory of ALLAH: for He is

The Exalted in Might, the Wise.

Dedication

This book is dedicated to my youngest son, Qa'id Jawwaad Salaam, and all the other men and women who have been imprisoned way beyond guilt.

Holy Qur'an

Surah 1.

Al Fatihah (The Opening)

1. In the name of ALLAH, Most

Most Gracious, Most Merciful

2. Praise be to ALLAH,

The Cherisher and Sustainer of the Worlds;

3. Most Gracious, Most Merciful;

4. Master of the Day of Judgment.

5. Thee do we worship,

   And Thine aid we seek.

6. Show us the straight way,

   7. The way of those on whom

     Thou hast bestowed Thy Grace,
     Those whose (portion)
     Is not wrath, And who go not astray.

QUID PRO QUO – a Latin phrase that means making a certain kind of deal: you do this for me, and I'll do this for you.[1]

"The truth is, the courts wanted Qa'id to snitch on someone else in a totally different case, **and in return**, Qa'id would be given a lesser sentence in the case he was arrested for. I was told by a prosecutor that **'This is ... _DONE ALL THE TIME_.'**"

-**excerpt from ...** _DONE ALL THE TIME._

---

[1]https://www.vocabulary.com/dictionary, Retrieved January 19, 2021

Editor's Note

The letters shared in this book are written by Qa'id Salaam's own hand during his incarceration. They are in his own words, his sincerest thoughts and feelings, and therefore, have not been edited in order to maintain his voice and authenticity. It is the author's desire that the reader looks past the grammatical errors to see the heart of the man who survived the judicial status quo of it's "... *DONE ALL THE TIME.*"

Life Outside of Prison

As Salaam Alaikum, (Peace Be Unto You) … I am now writing from the OUTSIDE OF THAT MAN'S PRISON. I was kept in HELL for over 13 years. I finally made it HOME! The mental battle in there is over, or should I say it has just begun out here. It's time for me to put into action the positive resources that I have acquired inside that guided me out of that MAN'S PRISON.

First, I WANT TO THANK *ALLAH*, for blessing me with another chance at life in the Real World. Allah guided my mother and gave her strength to push for my early release for many years, and finally through an Excellent Program; called "Beyond Guilt" – Ohio Justice & Policy Center, this Compassionate Non-Profit Program from the great mind of Attorney

David Singleton, I was acquitted of a crime, but I had to plead guilty to another crime that I was never tried for nor found guilty of. "Quid Pro Quo." I believe these new accusations were done by the courts to save the face of the courts and to avoid paying me for wrongful incarceration.

This program was unveiled April 26, 2019, to help guilty incarcerated prisoners by reducing excessively long sentences.

"If the country is ever going to get serious about reducing mass incarceration, David Singleton says criminal justice reform must begin to address the issue of people in prison who've been over-punished and are serving excessively long sentences. Beyond Guilt is our answer to criminal legal system reform that focuses narrowly on the lower-hanging fruit of the reform movement-freeing innocent prisoners and people convicted of low-level non-violent offenses", Singleton says.

I was granted early release, "Time Served", on January 28th, 2020 from an original sentence of 18 years to life. *ALLAH* works for those who are Steadfast and Pure in Heart. I know *ALLAH* feels my heart.

Even though I lost appeal after appeal and my continuation of Pro-Se-Motion, MY MOTHER NEVER GAVE UP. She would search for new resources to bring to the table until she was lead to the "Beyond Guilt Program" through word of mouth. For awhile I thought I would never make it home. I feel my mother had a plan that she heard straight from *ALLAH*.

I got locked up at the young age of 19, now I'm 32 years old. I am PROUD to say I'm a changed man, I grew up in prison. I feel

ALLAH has chosen me to help everyone I can, to better themselves, through a program I was selected to facilitate while in prison called, "Thinking For A Change."

This is a Critical Thinking Program I facilitated while in prison too many inmates. I'm certified to facilitate this program in and outside of prison. The institution I was in was chosen to launch this pilot program and I was one of 12 out of 300 plus inmates selected to facilitate," Thinking For A Change" inside the institution.

As of today I am the first to be released from prison to be honored to facilitate this program outside and inside of the institution. My goal for this self-help initiative is to deter youth in high schools from walking in my shoes, and going to prison. I think it would be even more beneficial to keep those in high risk from going to prison. This is my way of giving back.

I will continue to Pray for all the men and women behind bars, especially those unjustly accused and have excessively long sentences.

I hope and pray that *ALLAH* has mercy on them, and he blesses and guides those inmates as he has blessed and guided me.

Qa'id

CHAPTER ONE

MY SON

I have an *incredible* husband, a REAL gentle man in every sense of the word. I'm writing this book after 43 years of marriage and I still can't get enough of his presence. Our journey has been an adventure and a blessing from the very beginning.

Thirty-three years ago, when I became pregnant again for the fifth time, I became very angry with myself. Before this pregnancy, I didn't understand how anybody could not feel blessed to have a new baby. There are so many women that can't conceive their own babies; and yet with this pregnancy, I was not mentally, emotionally, spiritually nor physically receptive. I started to think to myself that maybe GOD was trying to let me know that all pregnancies weren't always happy ones. I can remember taking some toilet paper and shoving it as far as it would go up my vagina, looking for anything RED! Later, I realized this must be a teaching moment for me; you see, I had been teaching Childbirth Education and Fertility Awareness for over four years. I used Fertility Awareness to get pregnant and not to get pregnant. This birth control worked for me for years. I thought to myself, "We obviously had sex one day too far into my cycle." Upset at this revelation, I called my fifth child my LUST child throughout the entire pregnancy.

With that being said, we already had four children: Three daughters and a son. Also, I was going to be turning 38 right before this child would be due, and right before my 20th high school reunion, which was three weeks before my due date. I was very perturbed.

My husband and I were coming up on 10 years of marriage, and he commented, in shock just like me, "I was wondering if this baby is mine." He was joking, of course; but, I was not in the mood for joking. I WAS PISSED. I responded, "SHIT! I WONDER IF IT'S MINE!"

The first person I told was my mother. I'm sure I told her in such a way of saying please be empathetic, and of course, she was kind. Then we called my husband's parents. His father was not too happy. As a matter of fact, he emphatically said, "Man, ya'll gonna have to get a room at the Y (YMCA)." I think he said that because he used to work there and that's what he saw. His mom was very gentle and said, "It will be alright."

One thing that got to me at that time was being pregnant at the same time as four of my nieces. They could have been my children. I was 38 years old! All but one had their babies before me. I couldn't celebrate their babies the way I wanted to as a great-aunt.

Of course, other people felt the need to put their two-cents in. My dearest brother said, "Damn, girl. Again?!" I thought to myself, "You got four children by three different women and you've been married five times, and not once did I say to you, 'Again?!' I always said, 'I hope you are happy ... AND furthermore, all of our children belong to me and my husband. We are happily married, and we never asked you to take care of one of them."

I told him off all in my mind!

That summer, my husband and I attended a neighborhood fair when an old acquaintance saw me and said the most ridiculous thing to me. It struck a sensitive nerve. She said, "I thought you said you and your husband weren't going to have any more children." Without hesitation, and out of frustration of being pregnant, I responded, "WE AIN'T STOP F---IN'!" I felt sorry for her; not really.

When it came time for my 20th high school reunion, I was big as a house trying to look as cute as possible. An old classmate saw me and said loudly, "Somebody finally slowed your fast ass down!" I could not bring any more attention to myself; but I was thinking, "You low-life crack head. You got a nerve. Get a Life." Instead, I smiled and said, "Good to see you, too."
She would eventually die of a drug overdose a few years later.

We never wanted to know the gender of any of our other children before they were born. My husband and I didn't think it was necessary and we liked the element of surprise. However, because I was older during this pregnancy and my blood pressure was a little high, I had my first ultrasound.

We were asked if we wanted to know the sex of our baby. I said why not? It is what it is. We learned that we were having another son. Sounded great. His brother would be glad.

It was September 7, 1987, Labor Day, when my contractions started, then stopped. False labor. Our day went on as planned: cooking, grilling, having a nice time with family and friends. It wasn't until early the next morning my water broke. Of course, we planned to have this baby at home, as we did with our other children, with the exception of our second child who was born prematurely in the hospital.

I had help with the grilling and fixing a nice Labor Day cookout. Early the following morning my amniotic sac (water) broke. I walked in circles around the dining room table as my mother-in-law mopped up the fluid that ran down my legs onto the floor.

Then around noon, the contractions started again and just petered out. Unlike giving birth in the hospital, I was in full control. I could eat and drink whatever I wanted. I ate some leftover grilled lamb breast, corn on the cob, grilled sweet potatoes and iced tea. Eventually, labor picked up again around 4p.m. after I drank a whole bottle of castor oil.

I invited some family and friends over to witness my son's birth, but I only allowed the midwife, doula and my husband in the bedroom while I was in labor. A friend who took pictures and slides of the birth of my fourth child was also present. Not only did we take pictures of the birthing, it was also videotaped.

Even with this being my fifth time giving birth, I was not on top of my spiritual connection with this pregnancy. I would have been very pleased if I could have found out the day before that I was pregnant and then given birth the next day. I was older and just didn't want to be pregnant for nine months again. Like I said, I always wanted to adopt a son so my oldest son would have a little brother to grow up with. He got one the old-fashioned way, instead. I remember thinking this child is going to have to go for himself in life because I'm tired.

Around 9:45 p.m. I sent for my birth witnesses to come up to my bedroom. I can still remember the looks on some of their faces.

Having never been present at a home birth before, they were truly nervous.

I recall glancing at the clock, it read 10:05 PM. Upset that I hadn't given birth yet, I started to think to myself, "I can't still be pregnant at 10:30PM!" I was so tired. Not long after those thoughts, it was time. My body started pushing the baby down. I pushed three or four times before his head crowned, and at that moment, I was more worried about how big my baby's head was going to be, if I'd tear or need stitches because his brother before him, his head felt like the biggest head in this world. I remember thinking when I was pushing my first son's head out, "I can't wait to tell this baby about its head." I thank merciful *ALLAH* that after pushing out Qa'id's head, it was not as bad as I envisioned, no tear or stitches.

After such a long day of laboring, I no longer had the will or the desire to push the rest of my baby out. And it seemed he was tired, too, because my baby's head hung out of the birth canal with no desire to come out any further. I heard my mother say, "Come on, baby." Then suddenly, and with little effort on my part, the rest of my son's body shot out so fast and my husband was right there to catch him, while being startled at how fast the baby came out.

All of our children emerged into this world without medication, and I felt every ounce and every inch of them. Our last child was no different. So, on September 8, 1987 at 10:29 PM, my "lust child" was born 21" long, weighing 7lbs 1oz. We named him Qa'id ("Leader", one of the names given to *The Prophet Muhammed,* PBUH) , Jawwaad

("Generous", meaning, *ALLAH* the Most Generous.) I gave him that name because his head was not as big as I thought it would be.

Three of my children were also present. Our five-year-old daughter was just too sleepy to stay up. Our 11-year-old and oldest daughter got very emotional and started to cry after the birth was all over. When I asked her why she was crying, she said "My stomach hurts." I guess she was sympathetically helping me push the baby out.

I have always thought what happens to a baby in utero is very important to his or her life. Being a doula and childbirth educator, I believe every child is affected by all influences during its development from conception to the very beginning of life and through childhood. As Qa'id got older, I would often reflect on his emergence into this world, and how he stopped or hesitated before coming into this world. It was a prelude to how he would live his life: stopping or hesitating before continuing his journey. I remember saying during my pregnancy that this child will have to go for himself, knowing that *ALLAH* was in charge. That has been the way he has lived. He smiled all the time, even when it would tell on him.

Not long after I gave birth to Qa'id, postpartum depression set in. My body went through changes that were very unfamiliar to me, and unlike the births of my other children, my body, spirit and mind were not totally committed to giving birth. My breathing became labored; I was perspiring heavily; and I had heart palpitations that felt as if they would never stop. Two hours later, I went to the hospital. When I arrived at the hospital I had a problem lifting my leg, I did just have a baby ya'll. The nurses offered no assistance, I was told to get up on the bed, a real problem, I could not manage having just given birth two hours earlier so, my husband helped me.

As my husband helped me get up on the bed, the first nurse started to take my blood pressure, while another nurse began taking my pulse. At that time, it seemed like something came over my body and my heart rate and pulse went back to normal. I checked in and out in less than 2 hours. I was released and ready to go home, only to be told to rest. Needless to say, I was ready to go home, because I wanted to breastfeed my baby.

Later on, that same day, the pediatrician came to give Qa'id his first baby checkup. She wanted us to take him to the children's hospital to have his jaundice levels checked. So, off to the hospital we went, and yes, his levels were jaundice. His Bilirubin Test was very high.

Qa'id was admitted to the hospital on the spot and put under the ultra-violet lights to break down the Bilirubin in his liver. Sometimes newborns can't break down the bilirubin because of the immature liver. He was there for four days. His bilirubin levels went down. He came home only to be readmitted the next day; his levels had gone back up, another depressing two more days. I was so relieved when his levels dropped and stayed down.

Even though I had him at home, we spent the first week of his life in the hospital. I was totally worn out and I still had four other children at home who needed my attention. Also, our tenth wedding anniversary was on the 10th of September, two days after Qa'id's birth. The gifts for ten years are either tin or aluminum, soft metals that demonstrate the toughness and durability of a couple's relationship and their devotion to each other. That year, my husband and I celebrated our tenth wedding anniversary in a hospital coffee shop. We Thanked *Allah* for our many blessings and prayed over a deluxe cheeseburger, crispy fries and a soda. For dessert, I brought from home, some homemade pound cake wrapped in aluminum foil.

This after birth experience was reminiscent of when I gave birth to my second daughter who was prematurely born and afflicted with a multitude of problems right after birth. By that I mean the time I spent alone in the hospital was a memory bought back to me when Qa'id had to be admitted and re-admitted for his bilirubin problem. Only a mother would be tested with that.

During my pregnancy with Qa'id, my blood pressure was slightly elevated. It never has returned to normal. This sometimes happens during pregnancy when you are older. You are categorized as a high-risk pregnancy. So, three months after I gave birth to Qa'id I had to go cold-turkey and stop nursing him because of the medication given for hypertension could cause harm to the babies liver. This was very hard for me, it seemed he adjusted better than me.

Postpartum depression is real, and it can be experienced in a lot of unpredictable ways. Antepartum depression which is similar to Postpartum depression (one during pregnancy the other right after pregnancy) they're both real, and it can be experienced in a lot of unpredictable ways. You may wonder what all this has to do with the relationship of my son and myself, and how things progress over the years. I really believe, as I said before, sometimes how you come into this world can be indicative of how you might live in it.

HIS YOUTH

From an early age, Qa'id was a sociable child with an infectious smile that showed through his eyes. I used to call him "Al Schottlkotte" after an old TV news reporter because he was so nosey and always wanted to be in the know. At an early age, Qa'id showed signs of being a serious leader. In kindergarten, Qa'id and his classmates dressed up as Pilgrims and Native Americans for a Thanksgiving play they put on for the parents. Qa'id, dressed as a pilgrim, smiled throughout the whole play, seeming to enjoy it until one of the parents came in right before the play was over. Qa'id's teacher asked the class if they wanted to do the play again for the benefit of the late parent who wanted to record it. Everyone screamed yes, except, Qa'id. He screamed "NO!" When his teacher asked him why he didn't want to do it again.

Qa'id loudly replied, "WE DID IT AND IT WAS STUPID!" I was so embarrassed. Qa'id was not going to budge nor change his mind.

As parents, we lived for our children. We lived in a large house, they loved having their own space along with the dog. My husband and I were very much involved in our children's activities, from karate classes, little league football, ballet, soccer, drill teams, to science programs at the university college campus. Whatever it was, we were there.

As a family, we played all kinds of games; mostly during the winter when they couldn't go out of the house. We had fun being together. When our children were young we celebrated Kwanzaa every year and observed our traditional Islamic days of Eid. Also we went on family trips at least once a year. We would go back East to see their paternal family. We would visit Atlantic City Beach and Wildwood Beach. We visited The White House and everything else in DC. We also went to the home of Martin Luther King Jr. in Atlanta, GA, and took a family trip to Disney World in Orlando, FL. We loved going to family reunions out-of-town. Our family did more together than most of the other families on our own street.

I still have a small valentine card Qa'id gave me when he was 9 years old. It has two lions on it and says, "C'mon … let's walk on the wild side!" I often thought about this card over the years in reference to his life's journey. It truly has been on the wild side.

When Qa'id was around 14 years old, he loved hanging out late at night with his friends.

At that time in our city, there was a 10 PM curfew for children under the age of 17. One night, the doorbell rings and it's the police. He says, "Is this Qa'id's residence?" I said, yes. The officer then told me that he was bringing my son home for curfew violation. I looked into the police car and sure enough, there was my son with about five other teens, male and female, sitting with his hands handcuffed behind his back and a big grin shining through his eyes. I just said, "I told you what was going to happen if you kept on doing what you are doing."

In May 2003, Qa'id finally graduated from the 8th grade. He was 15 years old. He was also the Class President, being one of the oldest in his class and a leader.

Qa'id's middle school and high school years were difficult. He enrolled in several different kinds of curriculum schools but never graduated from any of them.

In the first two weeks of high school, Qa'id tried out for the reserve football team where his older brother was a well-known player on the varsity team. One day, after practice, Qa'id decided he didn't want to wait on me to pick him up, so, he stole someone's bike and rode it home. His actions caused him to get kicked off the football team and be put out of the high school. Qa'id straight up lied about it to his father and me, and we believed him.

He told us that someone he knew loaned him the bike, which was a total lie. Yes, we believed him, we had no reason not to. I should have remembered the letter he had written me some years earlier about why he lies. Anyway, we tried for a few weeks to find this non-existing person. The school's police officer told us as politely as he could, that Qa'id was lying. I really don't like to be lied to! I didn't ask you to lie to me.

Shortly after this happened, Qa'id was picked up for trespassing at the same school he was kicked out of. This landed him in a juvenile detention center. I thought it was ridiculous. When I was in school, if a student trespassed, they were told to leave, not given a juvenile criminal record at sixteen, like my son.

Treasure the hardships you go through to protect your own.
GODS Grace awaits them. You must be Patient. Those with Patience always win. Patience is hard but is fruitful with GOD's help.

FAMILY

TRIP TO PHILADELPHIA

ATLANTIC CITY, NJ

QA'ID'S 8th BIRTHDAY

QA'ID AND
KARATE TROPHIES

QA'ID the ATHLETE

QA'ID SCHOOL DAY

QA'ID and SIBLINGS

All About "Living That Life"

By the time Qa'id was 17 years old, we knew he was not living right. One day, he was standing across the street from our house, in front of the bus stop, with two other male teens when all of a sudden, Qa'id and one of the guys, ran into the house and went upstairs. A few seconds later there was a hard knock on the front door; It was the police. When I answered, he asked where the boys were that had run in and went upstairs. I asked why? The police officer said that they had a gun. I said, "WHAT?!" The officer asked if he could search the house. First, I said "No!", but then he said he would wait in his car until he got a search warrant, so I said OK. I agreed to let him go upstairs.

One reason why I was hesitant to allow the officer to go upstairs was because I heard of cops planting things in people's houses. The other reason was that my daughter was moving out and her things were all over the upstairs hall and her room. I went upstairs with him. He looked everywhere and in everything, making more of a mess. When he didn't find anything, he left. I was livid at my son. I didn't find out until years later that they actually did have a gun, but the officer just couldn't find it.

A couple months later, my husband pulled in the driveway to see Qa'id and his friend smoking marijuana on the front porch. A loud altercation occurred. Qa'id was being so disrespectful. His dad was so upset, he was shaking. This was told to me by my sister, who had come to visit us that day. I was not home. My husband was not a street person at all. He really thought he could reason with his son, but he couldn't that day, so, he called the police on his own son. I was furious, wondering how could he do that? My heart was so heavy. How could he put his own son in the system when I have been trying for years to keep him out of the system. I know in his own way my husband was trying to help our son; but, because of his disobedience and disrespect, Qa'id landed in juvenile court. Unfortunately, this changed nothing on his journey to self-destruction.

I didn't know my son, my lust child, my baby boy. It felt as if it was us against him, as if overnight, our son's life was changing from sugar to shit. The path he had chosen was leading him straight to pain for all of us. He was running away from us and the path we deemed as straight.

Qur'an

Sura 19, Ayat:77

Hast thou then seen

The (sort of) man who

Rejects Our Signs, yet

Says: I shall certainly

Be given wealth and children.

As parents, we were trying to lead by example. We didn't pretend we were perfect, but we disciplined our children and tried to show our children love and respect. They didn't witness any child or spousal abuse. They were punished when it was called for. In my Childbirth classes, I would say all the time that it would be much easier on a parent if Allah had attached a book to each baby's umbilical cord on how to raise that particular child.

We were involved in our children's lives. We taught them our family history, and "Black History" was taught all year around. As a family we went to our religious place of worship and we tried to lead by example. We surrounded our children with like-minded people. Qa'id rejected everything we were about because he preferred trying to live *that life*. He flat out told me he wanted to be a gangster. I laughed and said, "No, you don't." He smiled and said, "Yes, I do." This was funny to me, because when he was in the 6th grade, he told me he wanted to be a police officer. Apparently, the criminal life was more appealing to his psyche. He liked the excitement.

There were times when my heart would sink when I was with my son. One day I happened to run into him on the street, so I picked him up. He was so much fun to be around, always smiling. We were talking and laughing about something when I slapped his leg. The laughter instantly stopped replaced by nervousness when I felt a big gun! I hit a gun. Instinct made me quickly pull over to the curb. I said, "You and your gun can get out." I didn't care where he went either. I felt Satan was after me, but Satan was chasing him, and I was not going to get caught with him.

A few months earlier, Qa'id walked into our dining room with a hand full of money as far as his hands could stretch … dollar bills ya'll … it scared the shit out of me! He said "here", giving it to me. I backed up, smiled and said, "If you get a real job, I swear, I will take every dime you get, as bad as we need money, but you are not going to tempt me with that. Give it to your dad." I knew how his dad was going to react. So, later that day, I asked his dad if Qa'id showed him the money. He said, "Yea, and I told him, 'Take your money and leave.'" This was the first time we put Qa'id out of the house. This was a test we both rejected. I felt if we had taken the money, we would be condoning how he chose to live.

In 2006, Qa'id turned 18 years old, all of our other children graduated from public high schools, but with our fifth child, we endured an uphill battle trying to get him to change his priorities for his future. He attended at least three charter school programs, completing none of them. If he had done what he was told he would have gotten a diploma and graduated that June.

Our oldest daughter was friends with a prominent manager of a well-known musician in Atlanta, GA who said he would take Qa'id in and mentor him. As a family we thought it would be best for him to move there. We were getting him ready to move down to Atlanta. We bought pants, shirts, socks and underwear and other personal things getting him ready to move to Atlanta. His suitcase was packed with all new clothes, waiting for the day Qa'id would begin his new journey. We weren't in a hurry. We thought as soon as he graduates, he will be on his way.

November 27, 2006 was the beginning of an unbelievable journey our family would experience; one that I would not wish on any soul; but at the same time, I must admit it saved my baby boy's life and made us who we are today. We learned a lot about what it meant to have patience and faith.

*Those who don't have Allah's approval
certainly don't have mine!*

The Qur'an

Al-Anfaal (8:14)

*Thus (will it be said):
Taste ye then of the (punishment).
For those who Resist Allah, is
the penalty of Fire.*

It was Easter Sunday, April 16, 2006. We invited a friend and her husband over for dinner. As we were enjoying each other's company, the phone rang. It was our oldest son. He said, "Ma, my friend just called me and said Qa'id just got shot in a Burger King parking lot and he's at the hospital!" At my distress at hearing this news, my thoughts immediately went back to a conversation Qa'id and I had two days earlier.

I was driving when my cell phone rang. It was Qa'id. He said I had just passed him at the Burger King parking lot. I turned my car around and picked up my baby. I had been missing him. He got into the car smiling, looking like a homeless derelict child. I wanted to steal him and take him home with me to be safe; but instead, we sat in my car and talked.

"Qa'id, what are you doin?"
"I'm alright", he said, smiling.

Frustrated with his nonchalance, I pointed to an insurance agency directly in back of where we were parked.

"You need to go back there and get yourself some life insurance because we don't have any money to bury you."

Qa'id laughed. "What you mean, Ma?"

"Qa'id, you could get shot or go to jail."

"You don't think my friends wouldn't get me out of jail?" was his reply.

"No! You could be maimed and we not even know about it."

My son, ever smiling and laughing, asked, *"What's maimed?"*

I continued to plead my case as we debated a little more, but to no avail. Before he got out of the car, I told him I loved him and wanted him to have a good life. He said, "I love you too, Ma."

That was two days before that fateful call.

Our friends drove us to the hospital. We could have passed the spot where Qa'id had been shot, but he drove down a street before that. We were spared the vision of seeing our son's blood senselessly pooled on the ground. Thanks to Allah, we don't have that as a memory especially since the lot is right next to the house that Qa'id was born in.

When we arrived at the hospital, the emergency parking lot was full of cars and people. I would learn later that it had been a drive-by shooting. Four teens were shot. Qa'id was one of them. The emergency room was chaotic. Victims of the shooting and their family members filled the place.

I was not familiar with any of the victim's family, nor did I know any of the other victims.

I heard one of the other victims' mother cursing up a storm. It was like looking at a movie of a hospital scene after a crime had been committed, and I was in the middle of the movie.

My husband and I were led into a small room where we had to show our ID's to get in. We waited in that room for what seemed like forever to see our son.

I felt so scared, nervous and helpless. It was like I had hit the lottery for statistics of black-on-black crime. No one was telling us if our son was dead or alive.

We prayed.

"Oh Allah, please protect our son. Grant him Your favor and help us to accept Your way."

What else could we do or say!

My husband, our oldest son and I were finally led through the doors to where our son was laying on a table. My heart was in my throat. I was angry and emotionally numb. My reaction and the expression on my face must have been obviously intense. I can remember the social worker saying to me, "You are really angry." I told her I was because I had just talked to Qa'id about this.

As we were walking back to him, I heard a doctor coming from the back, loudly saying, "YOU BLACK BOYS JUST DON'T KNOW WHAT YOU ARE DOING TO YOURSELVES!" You could tell he had seen his share of young black boys coming through the ER shot up.

We didn't know what to expect when we got back there. I was glad to see my son's eyes open, but he couldn't move. He had been shot in the back and the bullet was still there.

Thanks to *Allah*, he was not paralyzed. A bullet had also passed through his right forearm, splitting it wide open. We couldn't see it because it was wrapped up. I thanked *Allah* that he was alive!

His brother screamed at him, "WAS IT WORTH IT?!" My oldest daughter joined us. She couldn't stop crying, just like she did on the day he was born.

Qur'an, An-Nissa (80)
He who obeys the messenger, Obeys Allah, But if any turn away, we have not sent thee to watch over their (evil deeds).

This shooting experience puts us in a group of statistics that no parent wants to be a part of. *All Praises Due to Allah.* No one died that night. I went through a range of emotions from embarrassment to gratefulness.

There was a detective walking around in the ER questioning the shooting victims. He asked Qa'id if he knew who had shot him. Strangely, Qa'id said, "Ask your boys. They were there. They saw everything. I got shot in the back." I thought to myself, "Oh, come on, Qa'id! He's only trying to help you." Qa'id knew why he said what he said to the detective. I didn't have a clue. I couldn't say anything. I was so scared I'd make things worse.

By this time, we were getting calls on our cell phones from many of our family members and friends who found out about the shooting and came to the hospital. We met them outside to give information on Qa'id's status. We shared our hurt and shock with them. The first faces I saw were those of my best friend's two sons who used to live with us and practically grew up in our house. I was still full of anger when I walked up to them and said as forceful as I could, "DON'T TAKE YOUR MOTHER THROUGH THIS SHIT!"

As fate would have it, both of her sons would die from gunshot wounds some years later, which made my friend a part of what I called the "Statistical Black Mama Syndrome."

The other three teen victims were released from the hospital that night with gunshot wounds to their arms or legs. Qa'id was injured the worst so he was admitted to the hospital. He was shot twice: once in his right forearm and once in his lower back. The doctor said the bullet was too close to his spine to try to remove it. They were afraid he would become paralyzed if they tried. So, as a result, the bullet is still in his lower back.

I guess I had taken my perspectives on gunshot victims straight out of TV and the movies. I'd envisioned when I visited him in the hospital the next morning there would be at least one detective outside his room. Not so I walked right in his room. I felt a little insecure and scared. The atmosphere was like he was in there for having a splinter in his foot removed. There was nobody around! It seemed the doctors and nurses didn't take his injuries as seriously as I did. I mean, he did have a bullet in his back, ya'll!

Again, it's "... *DONE ALL THE TIME*!"

I was told he was going to be released from the hospital that day and I would have to make clinical appointments for follow-up care for his back and arm. So, out the hospital door we went, one day later, with pain pills and a bullet in his back, and without ever talking to the police. I didn't know how to feel or what to think. I wondered if the person who shot my son was still looking for him to finish the job. Did they know where we lived or would some nut come by and shoot up our house? There was no advice from the police. We were left to feel that we had to *live at our own risk* with a child that didn't seem to take all this drama seriously. I felt like a traumatized victim. Needless to say, we could not send Qa'id to Atlanta, or anywhere else, due to his injuries and my mental state!

Now that our son, Qa'id, aka Q-Streetz, his street name, was home from the hospital, a few of his friends stopped by to check on him. They were all glad to see him alive. Q-Streetz acted very cocky, laughing and still playing the role of a dangerous gambler with his life. It's sad because as a family we were knee deep in his shit too.

"Those who act blindly will pay for their weakness."

Qa'id was expected to graduate the following month, but due to his injuries and being unable to keep up with his schoolwork, he had to sit out the remainder of the school year. The nerve damage in his right arm and hand kept him from using his right thumb. He was unable to write. A few months passed and Qa'id was back in school.

It's September 3, 2006, Labor Day weekend, and five days before Qa'id's 19th birthday, when I received a call. It was Qa'id.

"Ma, I'm at the hospital. I got shot in the leg. I'm alright." "Qa'id! What are you trying to do?!"

I could hear the smile in his voice as he tried to reassure me he was okay. I had to go pick him up from the hospital *again* but alone this time. My husband was emotionally done. Disgusted, he got in his car and drove off. I felt as alone and hurt that day as I did when Qa'id was admitted to the hospital as a newborn for jaundice.

The scene at the hospital was very different from the first gunshot incident. The ER parking lot was not full of family and friends and there weren't any ambulances or police cars present. The hospital staff seemed to go about their day business as usual. When I pulled up, I didn't need to go in to get him this time. Qa'id was waiting for me right inside the emergency room door. I didn't feel like I was picking up my son who just got shot, *again.* I felt like I was there to pick him up for treatment of a pimple busting, so nonchalant was his behavior.

As he walked out of the hospital, he was listening to a police officer. I heard her too because she was the one doing all the talking. She said she was told by a by-stander at the scene of the shooting that Qa'id, and the one who shot him, both had guns. He denied it. No charges and no investigation. That was the end of the conversation because Qa'id was not talking.

This experience taught me what the old saying, "Only a mother could love you", meant. I felt very much like I did when I realized I was pregnant, wondering if this was my child?!

I reflected on how I used to get very agitated with my mother when she would run after her youngest son, trying to help save him from his battle with his demons and crack addiction. This day became one of many that showed me the true meaning of a mother's unconditional love for her children.

I was once again perplexed as my mind immediately went back to the first gunshot episode. I don't think there is one mother that wants to think about someone trying to kill her child. Of course, I am wondering again if I'm in danger by picking him up and driving through the same neighborhood where he was shot, not once, not twice, but three times!

School started back in August 2006. Again, still trying to guide and make sure he LIVES and completes high school. Now, Qa'id was targeted to graduate that December.

CHAPTER TWO

TRUMPED-UP CHARGES

Our family had no idea what was coming next. We truly were not expecting the bomb of lies that was about to tear our family unit apart for over a decade. I could not leave my child hanging. I used to tell all my children, "DO NOT PUT YOURSELF IN THE HANDS OF OTHERS BECAUSE YOU MAY NOT LIKE THE CHOICES THAT THEY MAKE FOR YOU!"

I thought all the other days of Qaid's life was a test, but they were just a rehearsal for what was to come.

On November 22, 2006, my husband and I flew to Philadelphia for the weekend to spend Thanksgiving Day with his sister's family, and, to also attend his 30th high school class reunion. Having a return flight for the following Tuesday, we made plans to meet with one of my husband's childhood friends for lunch on Monday.

As we were saying our goodbyes, my cell phone rang. The caller was one of our dearest Muslim brothers, Wadu Wali. "I just saw your baby boy on the 12 O'clock News", he announced. The butterflies in my stomach caused me to want to go to the restroom. I held my breath and said, "For what?" He continued, "The news reporter said he was shooting at an undercover police officer!" I remember responding loudly, "This boy done lost his damn mind!" I couldn't tell you what else was said. My body and mind went to, "Here we go again." I was in shock I wanted to disappear from where we were. I couldn't get home quick enough, but our return flight was not until the next day.

My body was on automatic. I had to get to him. When we landed at the airport, we couldn't get through the airport terminals to pick-up our luggage quick enough. Everything seemed to be in slow motion. The ride home that evening was like coming home from a long road trip.

We weren't home 10 minutes when the phone began to ring off the hook. The telephone's answering machine was full of messages from family and friends. Some of the calls were just inquires, trying to figure out what happened. Then there were messages from a few of his friends, saying things like, "Qa'id didn't do that. He was standing with us" or "Next to me." Some of them told us they had witnessed the shooting.

What Do You Do First?

The next few days were a blur. My husband and I went down to The Justice Center the following morning where we thought Qa'id would be housed. We were told we wouldn't be able to see him because he hadn't been processed in yet, and he wasn't assigned a cell floor.

One of his friends, Ms. Eden, called me and said she would go with me to the police station to let them know it wasn't Qa'id who was doing the shooting. He was standing next to her. Ms. Eden and another one of Qa'id's male acquaintance, Mr. Gabe, said that they would go to the police station and tell them what they knew. I had never met either one of them. The next day, I picked them up and headed to the police station, feeling pretty good, thinking they will let Qa'id go because I had proof that he was innocent.

Boy, was I wrong! The detective literally laughed in my face and said, "Next time you bring a witness here, make sure they are not wanted." Ms. Eden had an outstanding warrant and was arrested on the spot. I wasn't sure why Mr. Gabe wasn't questioned. That puzzled me, but I found out later, who he was. I never saw Ms. Eden again.

Our first time seeing our son in jail was so heart breaking, I really tried to hold back the tears for his sake, trying to give him strength. We saw our son behind a glass-barred window. This scene was somewhat familiar to me because of TV and the movies. Words cannot describe how humiliating you are made to feel while you are visiting your loved ones who are locked up.

You are made to feel like you have committed the crime. From the moment we walked through the security detector to picking up the phone, waiting to hear our son's voice, until they cut off the connection, we were made to feel like we were prisoners in jail, too!

I remembered a time when my mother asked me to go with her to see my brother, the crackhead, when he was in jail for no child support because of his crack habit. I was very adamant when I refused to go with her. My mother said to me, "Well, I hope none of your children ever go to jail." Smugly, I thought to myself, "Uh, I hope not, too." But here I am. I should have been kinder to her. *KARMA,* as they say, is a *"B."*

Qa'id told me that when the shots were fired, everyone scattered. He ran into an apartment building across the street from the park and only came out when he thought it was safe to. At that moment, the police showed up and immediately arrested him. It was like the police had staked out the place and was waiting just for him. The news reporters were there filming him being put up against the police car with his hands cuffed behind his back. They also bagged his hands to be checked later for gun powder residue, which was never found. The police also checked him for a gun, none was found, thank God. Qa'id was also checked for money because he supposedly robbed someone. All he had on him was some change, not even one-dollar bill. There was no proof on him for what he was accused.

I often wondered that if we had the $250,000 needed to bail him out, would our lives be different today. Qa'id lived so recklessly we thought we'd have to plan a funeral, but *All Praises Due to Allah,* Qa'id had been given *another* chance to change his direction.

After Qa'id was arrested, we were told two different accounts of the incident. The first account was told to us by Brother Wadu Wali when he called us to let us know our son was arrested for shooting at an undercover police officer. The second account painted a different picture. Qa'id was arrested for robbery and for shooting his gun while running through a crowded park. We were never told who he allegedly robbed nor was there anything else mentioned about the charges of shooting at an undercover police officer. It just didn't make any sense to us. If the first story was true, I think my son would have been shot that day, on the spot. Shooting at an undercover police officer is a crime that most don't walk away from. He would've been history! I don't think I'm wrong. We learned later that it never happened. It was a made-up story to arrest Qa'id.

The truth is, the courts wanted Qa'id to snitch on someone else in a totally different case, and in return, Qa'id would be given a lesser sentence in the case he was convicted of. I was told by a prosecutor that "This is ... *DONE ALL THE TIME*." But That Don't Make It Right!

Our son would call home almost *every day*, sometimes more than once a day, the entire time he was locked up, and if I was home, I'd answer every call. For years I felt I was the only one home because *no one* but me would answer the phone when Qa'id called. At first, I didn't take it personally since I was the one paying for the calls; but, after a while, it became a nuisance. Qa'id would call often wanting to be placed on conference call so he could speak with family and friends, calls could last up to 20 minutes. It became disruptive and nerve-racking because I had to stay on the line to connect the calls to whomever he wanted to talk to. There were times no one would answer, or it would be a wrong number. Over the years, phone numbers changed quite often. There were those who no longer wanted to talk to him. It was indeed a nuisance at times, but I felt it was the least I could do for him, since I never thought he was guilty of the crimes he was accused of.

A lot of times, I would be very angry when his father seemed to not share my same sentiments; back to a mother love is always there.

I'm not saying his father didn't love him; of course, he did. He had his own way of staying strong. It was his pride that got in the way. I did not understand why my husband felt the way he did until I had a conversation with friends who had a son that was incarcerated. Talking with them gave me a better understanding of how fathers feel and the personal disappointments they experience when their sons are incarcerated. It was an attack on the pride they had as fathers. Mother's think differently than fathers. Mothers carry their babies for nine months and they will always be their babies, no matter what, ordained by *ALLAH*!

However, through a sanctioned program titled The Family Is First Program (TFFP), Qa'id and his father later broke through that father pride blockage and found peace by crying, hugging and forgiving. So many loved ones and inmates found their peace, too.

The Family Is First Project, founded and facilitated by Apostle Stacie Johnson, was a family program that played a healing role in breaching the communication gap between inmates and their loved ones. The prison Qa'id was in saw a need and allowed Apostle Stacie to conduct her program within its walls. For all involved, the program was what we needed. TFFP was so effective, garnering and effecting great change in inmates and their loved ones, that it ran for ten years in the same institution.

Qa'id was arrested November 26, 2006. It was now December and I was in a hurry to get our son out of jail. While visiting my son at the justice center, I ran into the same detective who mocked me about supplying witnesses with arrest warrants. We recognized and acknowledged each other but when I mentioned I was trying to get my son out of jail by Christmas, she again laughed and said, "Good luck with that." I was thrown by her response because I had witnesses to say Qa'id was not the perpetrator and there was no physical evidence to show otherwise. In fact, during a visit, an inmate walked behind Qa'id while we were talking on the phone. Qa'id pointed him out and said, "There goes the guy who they said was doing the shooting in the park." I asked my son if the police knew it was him. He said, yes. Hearing this, I thought they would have let him go. Without a specific date, Qa'id's court appearance was not scheduled until after the first of the year (2007).

Hardship and difficulties are our test as humans. The weak fail. The ones who believe in Allah will survive and succeed. If they only trust in ALLAH and only ask him for help. Allah wouldn't leave them helpless. Faith and Blessing.

***

The-Made Up-Story

The Grand Jury decided to throw my statement
out of court. They didn't like what I had to say,
because I told them I had nothing to do with the
crime in another murder case, and I didn't
know anything about it. I was offered a Plea
Deal, at that time I didn't understand what that
meant to my case, I was only 19 years old, but
supposedly I would have gotten less time in this
case I was accused of ... I WAS PUT ON
TRIAL WITH A CO-DEFENDANT and WAS
GIVEN THE SAME SENTENCE HE GOT ...
the questions the Grand Jury wanted me to
answer, had nothing to do with the crime I was
put on trial for and did time for. I was asked
questions about a totally different crime. When
I kept saying I didn't know anything about that
crime and I wasn't there, I think I pissed
somebody off, and got the door slammed in my

face with another crime. The plea bargain was to tell The Grand Jury that a childhood friend killed a white man in a whole different case. I had no first-hand information about this killing.

"... DONE ALL THE TIME"   *Qa'id*

***

It is now the first of the year and I am told by his first public defender that Qa'id was a witness to a murder. This was new news to me. No one had ever mentioned to me before about a murder or that Qa'id had been accused and indicted for it. Not even Qa'id. I was in total shock. I thought she was going to tell me that my son was going to be released soon. Nothing was said about why he was still in jail.

On January 4, 2007, instead of what I thought was a continuation of the alleged charges against him (shooting at an undercover police officer, armed robbery and shooting in a public park), a new charge was brought against my son: Murder. I was baffled!

I wanted to scream, "WHAT IS THIS?!" What a low blow from the system, from the very people who made you swear to 'TELL THE TRUTH, THE WHOLE TRUTH AND NOTHING BUT THE TRUTH. SO HELP ME GOD" and they do this?! I felt like I had been Punk'd and Cat Fished. I took this new charge personally. They were charging my son for a crime he did not commit. After this, how can I believe anything they say? Especially since this kind of thing is ... *DONE ALL THE TIME*.

When I went to court for his arraignment, I overheard the prosecutor, Ms. Cromwell, say to the two detectives on the case, "Is that all you have?" leading me to think they didn't have anything pertinent against Qa'id. Ms. Mary Wilson, the first public defender in a different case, knew about this new charge against my son. She sat down next to me during his arraignment and told me that, "If he gets out of this, he can go home." That gave me hope. It didn't seem that they had much to charge him with since he was just a witness. I asked if she would defend Qa'id again, but she couldn't. She had other cases to work on. That was the last time I saw or spoke to her. Later, I thought she was just a part of the system.

The grand jury indicted Qa'id on 5 different counts:

Count 1 *Aggravated Murder with Specifications (SF), 2903-018 ORCN*

Count 2 *Murder with Specifications (SF) 2903-02A ORCN*

Count 3 *Murder with Specifications (SF) 2903-02B*

Count 4 *Aggravated Robbery with Specifications 2911-01A1 ORCN*

Count 5 *Robbery with Specifications 2911-02A2.*

(There had been a plea deal involved, also. I'll talk more about that later.)

As his mother, I knew nothing at all about this. Qa'id turned 19 years old the year before and the police were no longer required to keep me in the loop. I felt they had been plotting and planning for a couple months, keeping us at bay, while they got their ducks in a row. I felt tricked. What happened to the other charges? The charges that everyone knew about. Charges that were reported on the news. No one in our family or our friends knew about these new

76

charges. Murder was a serious charge and yet no one knew about it? It was not even reported on the news. These new developments took our lives to a whole new level. Now, I was thinking Qa'id went from a victim of being wrongly accused of robbery and shooting at an undercover police officer to a victim falsely accused of murder. There again, it's ... *DONE ALL THE TIME*.

My *GOD*, I questioned. Why me? Why us? How do you swallow and address these feelings! *Only through God's Grace and His Words, and A Loving Mother's Faith*! I thought of all the old cliché's: ... After Difficulty Comes Ease! ... In Every Cloud There Is A Silver Lining! ... God don't put no more on you than you can bare!

None of this made any sense to me. I thought that *ALLAH* must think I'm a very strong person, why else would he pick me for this burden? He must have something to show somebody besides me, because in my prayers, I would always ask Allah to use me as a *Muslim* so that others could learn from me. Deep down I knew it was my destiny, and I would do my best to past this TEST. So, I tried to put my fears behind me and said to myself, "Why Not?" Keep smiling and let *ALLAH* guide you!

My thoughts on the second public defender, Mr. Stewart, were that he was not concerned about proving Qa'id's innocence. Throughout the entire trial, he would say the same thing to me, "They have to prove he did it." He presented no defense at all for Qa'id. Personally, I thought there really wasn't anything to defend except the testimony of his co-defendant, Mr. Marco, and the made-up testimony of one of the detective's story of "he said, he said."

I had no idea how the court's processes or procedures worked, how a judge or jury was selected, or what a court docket was. But as it stood, Qa'id's trial was not presided over by Judge Means, the original judge appointed to the case, but by Judge College who was brought out of retirement. Judge G. Means' name was on all the paperwork and he made rulings in the case, but the case was heard by Judge College because Judge Means' docket was full. The case was moved to another court room and presided over by a retired visiting judge. I often thought Judge Means never even read Qa'id's case records at all. This was just my opinion, but I felt that the ruling from Judge Means on Qa'id's case could be crucial during his trial and in his appeals.

From the beginning, he ruled that Qa'id would be tried with a co-defendant, Mr. Lil'T. Even though his public defender, Mr. Stewart, tried to get Qa'id a separate trial, Judge Means refused to allow it. I learned later that if Judge Means had allowed a separate trial, there would not be a trial for Qa'id because it would then be a case of a co-defender's word against Qa'id's word. During the trial, this proved to be one of the biggest decisions this judge could have made.

Again, he was falsely arrested and accused in the case of shooting at the undercover police officer or robbery and shooting in the park. I suppose these charges were secretly dropped and never mentioned again.

Sometime later, it could have even been a few years, I went down to the courthouse records department to get all Qa'id's records. I was told that he didn't have any arrest records on file. I was baffled. How could someone get charged and indicted and be serving time in prison and not have an arrest record? Because …"IT'S ... *DONE ALL THE TIME*.

I learned about this senseless shooting on the same night it occurred because it happened the night of my third daughter's 24th birthday. I'll never forget it. My oldest daughter came home crying her eyes out. The young man who got shot, (I'll call him "Mr. Ahmed A.") was very close with my oldest daughter. They had gone to the same high school. She always referred to him and his brother as her big brothers. I never met Mr. Ahmed, or his brother Rick, but I had heard their names a lot.

I have to mention that some years later, Mr. Rick was having some issues, what they were,

I'm not sure. Mr. Rick killed his own mother, and the police killed him. My thoughts at that time were, I pray that what happened to his brother, Ahmed, didn't cause him to kill his mother, and commit "Suicide By The Police" (sooo sad).

He had been in jail six months before this murder trial started. During the trial, of course, Ms. F. Cromwell, the prosecutor asked a detective, so, "Mr. Qa'id is already in jail on another charge, right?"Of course, the answer was yes. This made Qa'id look guiltier. The detective was never asked the reasons why he was in jail or the fact that the initial arrest was bogus and was never addressed; it was dropped like it never happened. This is one of the reasons I said the public defender, Mr. Stewart, didn't defend him well, at all.

Picking the jury was very interesting, and there were a few who were excused. One jurist was hard of hearing, another jurist knew the defense lawyer's sister. There was a potential jurist who said she was a Born Again Christian, and that "Only *GOD* could Judge" … she didn't feel comfortable. Then there was the jurist who said her daughter was robbed and her nephew was in jail. Some jurists were very eager to serve. Those were the ones who scared me the most.

When the court was done picking the jury, the court selected one older African American female and one other middle age African American female as an alternate. There wasn't one African American male chosen to sit in the jury, and this was a jury of his peers? I think NOT!

"IT'S ... *Done All The Time*

When the jurist was sworn in, Judge College told them to pay attention and stay awake! It was obvious that some of them didn't have a clue about what their new job was going to encompass. I could say the same for all involved in this case. For instance, there were times when the trial got to be a little boring and some of the jurist would nod off to sleep. Even Judge College would nod a little; of course, he was retired (too old). That's what old folks do. I would not say this happens in all court cases, but in this case, it happened more than once.

I took notes during the trial. I remember thinking ... Do they realize they've got the lives of other people in their hands? I bet they won't remember half of what was just said.

Because of extenuating circumstances, the court had to make some changes on how the first witness would be called. The first witness, Ms. Terry R. had been deemed a star witness *and* a hostile witness.

She was also a victim the night of the shooting. She was sitting in her car and got caught in the cross fires, and a bullet grazed her arm which later was stapled closed.

April 24th, 2007, I arrived at the courthouse around 9:10am. I was in the long line outside the courthouse for over 20 minutes. When I got outside the courtroom, I passed Ms. Terry R. and her aunt in the hall. I could hear them discussing whether or not she would testify. There was another girl with them. She stated that she knew somebody who didn't want to testify, and they didn't. She said to Ms. Terry

R., "They can't make you." Ms. Terry R. had six days to go before her baby's due date.

The lawyers and the prosecutor prepared their table with stacks of papers and books. The prosecutor talked with the detective about how they would approach Ms. Terry R.

I could hear them talking about how they were going to bring down Qa'id and Mr. Lil'T (Qa'id's Co-Defendant #1). They discussed putting Ms. Terry R. in the jury room. The Prosecutor went out to ask if she wanted to go in the jury room.

When the prosecutor came back in, he stated, "She said she is 'staying right there', and that would probably be the last contact I will have with her. She seemed a little agitated."

At 9:50 am, Qa'id and his co-defendant, Mr. Lil'T were brought into the courtroom. As they loosened Mr. Lil'T's handcuffs, the court's secretary told the Judge everyone was there. Mr. Lil' T was Case A and Qa'id was Case B.

During the investigation, the detectives showed Ms. Terry R. an array of pictures that didn't include Qa'id's face.

When Ms. Terry R. testified, I found it to be one of the most important and the most incomplete testimonies during the entire trial. Even the way she was presented to the court was very stressful for her. You see, Ms. Terry R. was in her ninth month of pregnancy. The detectives had gone to the hospital and got her after she had been experiencing false labor. Her aunt came with her. Her baby was due in 6 days. If she had gone into active labor, the outcome of this trial would probably have gone a different way.

The courts needed her testimony and if she hadn't gotten on the stand, her testimony would have been videotaped.

She stumbled through her answers. I felt she had been badgered for her response, which made her very combative with her answers.

Judge College told her if she didn't come to court by 9am the next morning, she would be charged with Contempt of Court. You could see this really frightened her. Her expected due date was in 6 days. A baby's due date sometimes can be off by 2 weeks, and because I am a Childbirth Educator/Doula, I thought to myself, what if she has her baby tonight? So much stress on that young lady.

The next morning, Ms. Terry R. and her support person (her mother) were on time like Judge College had ordered. They sat on the bench right in front of me. She had no idea who I was. I didn't think it would be appropriate for me to introduce myself. She still seemed very nervous. When the detectives brought Qa'id and Mr. Lil' T into the court room, Qa'id walked in first. I heard Ms. Terry R. say to her mother, "I DON'T KNOW HIM. I AIN'T NEVER SEEN HIM BEFORE." My heart smiled for the first time since Qa'id had been in jail.

When Ms. Terry R. took the stand for the second time, she was asked if she recognized anybody from the night of the shooting. She said she recognized Mr. Lil' T from high school.

Ms. Terry R. didn't want to testify. You could tell she was very nervous. The Judge did a lot of small talk, trying to get her to connect.

She said, "I was told I wouldn't have to get on the stand."

She asked the Judge, "Don't I have a right to say I don't want to testify?" The Judge said, "I can fine you with Contempt of Court." He tried to explain what Contempt of Court was. The prosecutor asked Ms. Terry R. if she was there! She responded with, "I do have the right to an attorney, right?" The Judge called for a side bar. She set on the witness stand with her arms folded.

Mr. Lil' T's mother came in behind me with two young men. The Judge said he was going to call for a public defender for Ms. Terry R., so he sent Qa'id and Mr. Lil' T out of the court room. When the public defender arrived, court reconvened. The Judge asked Ms. Terry R. if she wanted to talk to the public defender. Her response didn't make any sense to me. She said, "I didn't get nowhere and basically I have no rights!" The Judge told Ms. Terry R. to "go on and tell us what happened on July 20th." Ms. Terry R. started to respond, "basically somebody got shot. I put my head down. How long can I be held in contempt?"

The following is a transcript of the line of questioning held between Judge Means and Ms. Terry R.:

Q: Do you understand the question?

A:Yes

Q: Where were you shot at?

A: In my forearm

Q: Did Mr. Lil' T shoot you?

A: They told me I didn't have to testify.

Then she was asked again

Q: Do you know Mr. Lil' T?

A: Yes, I went to high school with him. I don't know how many men it was doing the shooting.

10:08am

The judge called Ms. Terry's mom up to the front. He gave her a speech about justice. Her mother asked the judge if they were holding her daughter. The judge said he was calling for a public defender.

10:12AM

The Judge sent Mr. Lil'T and Qa'id out of the court room.

10:13 AM

My brother-in law came in the court room. I briefed him on what was going on.

10:15am

Qa'id's brother and third oldest sister came in.

Our third daughter came into court, she sat down next to me. She had taken off her blouse when I just so happened to turn around and read what she had written in Huge bold Letters, "PROOF" across the front of her tee-shirt. I said to her, "Cover that up and please put your blouse back on." I didn't want to draw any attention. She did, reluctantly.

10:50am

Right before Judge College called for a break, I noticed his head kept nodding. I mentioned this to Qa'id's lawyer, who said, "Don't worry about it." I didn't understand why I shouldn't worry. I was thinking, how much of the testimony did he miss?"

When court was back in session, we were moved to the back row so the jury could have seats to see the exhibit's better. A county sheriff said very rudely, and forcefully, "No cell phones. I don't want to see you texting or nothing." OK, maybe he saw or heard something. I didn't.

Ms. Terry R. was asked in all kinds of ways if she thought Mr. Lil' T did the shooting.

First defense lawyer, Ms. De-Ann, questioned Ms. Terry R.:

Q: Do you see the individual that you attended High School with?

A: Yes.

Q: Anywhere in the courtroom today?

A: Yes!

Q: Can you please point him out and describe what he's wearing for the record?

A: Blue Shirt.

Q: Well stipulated identification, thank you, so noted.

No more questions were asked of Ms. Terry R.

I thought for sure Qa'id's public defender, Mr. Stewart, was going to say something like, "Ok, Ms. Terry R. You say you recognize the one in the blue shirt, Mr. Lil' T, but do you recognize Mr. Qa'id in the white shirt?" Just that one question and answer could have set Qa'id free. I had already heard her say, "I don't know him. I ain't never seen him before!"

Ms. Terry R. was the star witness and the eyewitness and the hostile witness and neither the public defender, defense lawyers nor the prosecutor asked her anything about Qa'id. Eventually, Ms. Terry R. was dismissed without the court asking her anything about Qa'id. This system is rigged to tell *their* story. *It's* ... *DONE ALL THE TIME.*

A paraphrase from the *Qur'an:*

... And (the unbeliever plotted and planned,

    and Allah too planned, and the best of

    planners is ALLAH).

    The devil has many tricks and traps.

    What weapons can't be determined to not

    commit the sins you have repented for.
"As

    for the good deeds you are doing, do
them

    to death, and never give them up":

    May ALLAH strengthen our Faith and
our

    Bodies, May ALLAH protect us, from
those

    Who set Traps.

Existence is a school, everyone is a student,

and Allah is the only teacher.

He manifest his titles and test us,

everyone must pass their own exam.

Make your Ancestors blood Proud, and

*Make Yourself worthy of your Mother's
Milk.*

Mr. Steward gave the following opening statement at Qa'id's trial:

"There isn't going to be any eyewitness testimony with regard to Mr. Qa'id. There is not going to be any fingerprints, any footprints, DNA of any kind. There is no gunshot powder residue, or any gun. No physical evidence that comes back to Mr. Qa'id."

Mr. Marco, the third co-defendant in the case, had a paid defense lawyer, Mr. Hill, who stood against the wall while Mr. Marco gave his testimony. Mr. Hill seemed to counsel and coach Mr. Marco while he was on the stand because his testimony appeared to be rehearsed.

Mr. Stewart questioned the statement of a detective who stated, through hearsay, that Mr. Marco told Mr. T. Johnson that Qa'id did the shooting. I have a sworn affidavit from Mr.

Johnson that he never spoke to any detective regarding Qa'id's case. Mr. Marco T. is charged with murder with Mr. T. Johnson in a separate case.

Mr. Stewart continued …

The Story goes ...Mr. Marco T. and Mr. Lil'T met up with Qa'id at a neighborhood apartment party. Mr. Lil'T says, let's go buy some dope. Mr. Lil'T borrowed a gun from his friend. Qa'id had his gun, but Mr. Marco stated he didn't have a gun. Mr. Lil'T was playing, saying he was going to rob his connect. We were not able to find his connect.

Co-defendant, Mr. Marco T. talking… *the three of them, Mr. Lil'T, Mr. MarcoT. and Qa'id walked over to one guy sitting on the crate, who I believed to be Mr. Ahmed; another guy sitting in a picnic chair; a girl that was in a car and a guy sitting on the wall.*

Mr. Marco goes on to say, *Mr. Ahmed was fiddling with his cell, and Qa'id said a second time, who are you talking to? What are you moving for? Mr. Ahmed got up and started to run. I looked and seent him run to the street, and the next thing I know, he would draw the gun that was on the holster and started shooting towards our way. I hit the ground. I remember Mr. Lil'T running in front of me and grabbing the Mac11 and started shooting. But, before Mr. Lil'T started shooting when the guy ran to the street, Qa'id was already shooting.*

Mr. Marco was asked who was the first person to fire a gun? He replied, *Qa'id. That happened right when the guy started firing at us. I saw Qa'id and Mr. Lil'T firing a gun. Then we all ran the way that we drove in.*

We all got in the same car and drove away. We went back to our neighborhood. Mr. Lil'T dropped me and Qa'id off. We got a ride with another friend. Mr. Sonny D. drove us to another neighborhood where we dropped Qa'id off at.

Q., How do you know Qa'id,

A., He went to school with my brother.

Q., Now, do you, Qa'id and Mr. Lil'T , the three of you typically hang out together?

A., Mr. Marco said NO. That was the first time they actually met.

Q., So, you are friends with Qa'id and your friends with Mr. Lil'T, correct?

A., Mr. Marco says, *Mr. Lil'T asked me, and I told Qa'id to get involved. I told Qa'id to ride with us.*

Q., You told Qa'id what the ride was?

A., No, I told him to ride with us ... And he agreed.

When Mr. Marco was cross-examined by Ms. De-Ann, Mr. Lil'T's paid lawyer #1, he was asked to ID his co-defenders. He identified both of his co-defenders by the clothes they were wearing.

Ms. De-Ann asked, in what sounded more like a statement to Mr. Marco,

Q., you would agree with me that Mr. Lil'T, you would call him – what they call on the street, he's a dope boy?

A., Mr. Marco , Yes.

Ms. De-Ann continued, all right.

Q., You would agree with me that you and Qa'id would be what they call on the street, robbery boys?

A., Yes, ma'am.

Ms. Dee-Ann says:

Q., As you sit here right now, Mr. Marco, you're charged with two aggravated murders, correct? ...

A., Yes ma'am ...

Q., and you're looking at life for those, correct?.

A., Yes ma'am.

Q., and based on your cooperation, you might just be doing 14 or 15 years flat.

A., Yes, ma'am.

Q., So which body are you getting for free, Mr. Ahmed or Mr. Boyce?

Ms. Cromwell: Objection.

The Court: Sustained.

My oldest son tapped me on the shoulder to let me know that Mr. Marco's mother was sitting next to him. She said hi. I said hi. She wanted to talk to me in the hall. I said when they take a break. I guess it was taking too long because she left.

Mr. Stewart stated to Mr. Marco,

Q., So in exchange – as I understand here, Mr. Marco, in exchange for your testimony and cooperation, you're going to get some consideration?

A., Yes, sir

Q., Depending on how it all turns out?

A., Yes, sir

Q., You're going to get consideration on this aggravated murder, right?

A., Yes, sir.

Q., And consideration on the other aggravated murder?

A., Yes. Sir.

Q., And consideration in the concealed weapon? A., Yes, sir.

Q., And consideration in the aggravated robbery? A., Yes, sir

Q., And that trafficking in cocaine charge?

A., Yes, sir.

Q., So it's going to be a package deal?

A., Yes, sir.

Q., And you're interested in getting the best deal you can, aren't you?

A., That, and that I'm not going to go do some time for something I didn't do.

Q., And you're saying you didn't do this?

A., Yes, sir.

Q., Okay, Okay. That's what I thought. ... And then while you were there you meet up with Mr. Lil'T and another guy?

A., No, sir. Me and Mr. Lil'T walked over there together with a couple of other guys.

Q., Yes. ... All right. Because you really know Mr. Lil'T better than you know Qa'id don't you.

A., Yes, sir.

Q., You and Mr. Qa'id had a little beef, hadn't you?

A., Yes, sir. That was concerning him and my little brother, actually. ...Yes, sir. It was him and my brother, I'm going to defend my brother...

Ms. Cromwell again,

Q., Now, you were asked if you saw anyone go into anybody else's pockets ...

A., Yes. ...

Q., Right. Once you went down on the ground, were you able to see specifically, what Mr. Qa'id or Mr. Lil'T were doing?

A., No. The last thing I remember seeing was the guy firing at us, and Qa'id coming. I mean,

well, Mr. Lil'T coming kind of in front of me,
and then I hit the deck. ...

Q., And when at that time?

A., Yes. I was on the ground with a guy that
was on the crate.

Q., And he had already fallen?

A., Yes.

Q., Down to the ground?

A., Yes.

Q., But who fired the first that night?

A., Qa'id did.

Ms. Cromwell: Nothing further from the State.

Mr. Dee-Ann says:

Q., You're the one who brought Qa'id into this situation to meet up. You said before this, Mr. Lil'T and 'Qa'id didn't know each other?

A., right.

Q., You and Qa'id were fine at this time?

A., Right.

Q., And he went riding with you, no problem?

A., Right.

Q., All right. And you hit the deck, Mr. Lil'T was already running, right?

A., Right.

Q., Okay. Shots were being fired at that point, so nobody is going through anybody's pocket?

A., Right.

... Q., You didn't go there to rob anybody, right? ... A., Right.

Q., When you got there you weren't robbing anybody else, and nobody was robbing anybody, right?

A., Right.

Q., Just happened that your buddy Qa'id over here didn't like the way Mr. Ahmed spoke to him or looked at him or something, and Qa'id pulled out his gun? ... It was basically how the guy looked at Qa'id. And I guess he felt offended, and that's when he pulled out his gun. ... And there was something simply between Qa'id and Mr. Ahmed?

A., Right. But when we were together, it's like if one in something we are all in something. I guess that's when Mr. Lil'T started firing.

Q., And had you had your gun you would have started firing too?

A., Being in that position, yes.

Q., Yes. Okay.

Ms. Dee-Ann: Nothing further.

THE COURT: Thank you, Counselor.

Mr. Stewart?

Got you boxed in that corner all week.

Mr. Stewart: May I approach, your Honor?

THE COURT: Please do.

Mr. Stewart: Mr. Hill, you may want to follow this. If I could hand you, Mr. Marco.

RECROSS-EXAMINATION BY MR.
STEWART: Separate Statements

*Q. This is the transcript of your statement,
there, Mr. Marco, that you gave to the police
on December 13ᵗʰ, 2006. Do you recall that?*

A. Right. ...

*Q., Okay. And Line – line, let's see, so it makes
sense, Line 17 you said – are with me there,
Line 17? ...*

A., Right. …

*Q., You said: So next thing you know, Qa'id
pulled out his gun, who are you talking to,
whatever, and the dude froze. And I guess he
has a holster on him or whatever, because I
seen him moving but he got up and ran to the
street, and then he started shooting, pow pow,
pow and I hit the deck.*

Q., Right.

A., You said that?

A., Right.

Q., Okay ...

Investigator asked:

Q., so the man that was seated in the lawn chair, in this picnic chair? ...

A., Yes sir. ...

Investigator:

Q., Qa'id pulls the pistol on him? ...

A., Yes, sir. ...

Investigator:

Q., Says it was, like, you know, who is the bad guy now,

A., right? ... Basically. ...

And Mr. Marco,

Q., you said: Yes, sir? ...

A., Yes, sir. ...

Q., And Investigator:

And that's when the guy that was seated gets up and runs? You said: A., Yes, sir. ...

Investigator: Q., Did you see him pull a gun and fire it back?

A., No, sir. The next thing I seen, they run in the middle of the street. I heard the first pow, and I

looked and I just seen him aiming toward our
way. ... Q., Right. ... That's what you said?

A., Right.

Q., Okay. And then he gets up and runs away,
is that what the investigator says. And you said:
A., Yes, sir. ...

Q., Yes. ... Okay.

Public Defender Mr. Stewart, stated …

Mr. Marco is a co-defendant, but because he
turned state evidence, they called him an
accomplice ... he's a co-defendant, but you're
going to hear he is charged with another
murder, another felonious assault with a gun.
This guy doesn't go anywhere without a gun.
And he's the state witness.

Another State's witness, Mr. T. Johnson is
charged in another murder with Mr. Marco.

Great Witness. Killers. People charged with
murder. Mr. Marco charged with this murder
and another murder. Mr. Marco cut himself a
deal.

Mr. Stewart went on to say,

... because the gun casing got picked up before
Mr. Ahmed died, and the casings were taken to
the police cruiser, there was a rush to put the
bullets back where the detectives thought they
picked them up from, and they tried to mark it
off. After Mr. Stewart asked the detective ... you
picked up ten casing, would you agree that at
that point,

If we were to make the investigation just at that
point of what you picked up, trying to
determine who was standing where, firing what
weapon, has now been compromised.

Mr. Stewart: *Okay. That's all I have. Thank you.*

Apparently, neither the judge nor jury heard any of this.

Mr. Marco gave two different statements: one to the investigator and the other while he was on the stand. The statement he gave on the stand, he put his right hand on the bible, left hand up high and swore to tell the truth! Why couldn't Qa'id's public defender just say, YOU ARE TELLING TWO DIFFERENT STORIES, SO ONE HAS TO BE A LIE.

... And (The Unbelievers) Plotted and Planned, and the Best of Planners is ALLAH.

I wanted to say something so bad! That last testimony was harder to deal with than any of my laboring before giving birth. Later that evening, our Imam (Islamic leader) called from out of town to check on us. His call was good for my soul!

The next morning, I arrived early to the courtroom. When I entered, I heard a taped phone call from someone talking from jail. I didn't know who it was, but I was hoping and praying it wasn't Qa'id. On the call he was talking about somebody pointing a gun at him. I had to walk out; my stomach was feeling queasy.

While I was sitting out in the hall, one of the detectives on Qa'id's case came down the hall and went into the court room. I assumed she was going in to talk to the prosecutor, Ms.

Cromwell, about the other case that was due to start that day.

About 9:20 that morning, they bought in Qa'id and Mr. Lil'T. The taped conversation I heard earlier was replayed. On it, Mr. Lil T, whose voice could be heard on the tape, indicated that he could fire a gun. "I can't even shoot two guns at once. He pointed a gun at me and mine didn't even shoot. That was the first time I ever tried to shoot somebody; you know what I mean?"

I was so relieved to know it wasn't Qa'id's voice.

During the trial, there was a lot of questioning of the detectives who were on the scene right after the shooting. There was quite a bit of testimony regarding the bullet casings being removed from the scene. Right after the shooting, and after Mr. Ahmed was taken to the hospital, the detectives on the scene assumed it was just another shooting, nothing too serious, so, they picked up the bullet casings. Mr. Ahmed was shot in the abdomen and was still talking. When he was asked who shot him, he replied, "Fuck You." Ahmed carried a holster that held his roll of money, Marijuana, cell phone and his gun. The detective also stated this area has been described as a high crime area. Less than an hour after he arrived at the hospital, Mr. Ahmed died. His death brought in the homicide crew which prompted the police who initially picked up the casings to place them back as best as they could remember.

Another questionable testimony was that of one of the investigating detectives:

Q., So what was your next lead in the case?

A., We received information from another detective in our office that he may have a witness.

Q., And did you speak to that individual?

A., Yes.

Q., And who was that?

A., Mr. T. Johnson.

Q., You would agree with me, would you not, that other than Mr. Marco, there is no eyewitness testimony as to Qa'id's being involved in this incident?

A., Yes.

Q., The only link to Qa'id is through Mr. Marco, one of the co-defendants?

A., Yes.

Q., That Mr. Marco, that there is a deal with, correct? That's the same Mr. Marco?

A., Case consideration, yes.

Q., Yes. There is certainly no gun connected to Qa'id in this case?

A., No, just one gun recovered.

Q., No casings that take you to Qaid.

A., No.

Q., No prints, no DNA, no physical evidence?

A., That's true.

Mr. Stewart: *That's what I thought. Thank you.*

I found out later that Mr. T. Johnson, who was in jail at the time of the trial, was the co-defendant in the other murder case that Mr. Marco was indicated in.

Now, I was led to believe in movies and on TV shows like "Law and Order", that this testimony was called, "HEAR SAY" and was not admissible in court; but not one Public Defense Lawyer objected. It was definitely a case of "He said - He said - He said – He said." The Detective said, on the stand, that another detective in his office told him that Mr. T. Johnson told him, that Mr. Marco told him, that Qa'id, Mr. Lil'T and him were involved in this shooting. (HARD TO FOLLOW, RIGHT?!)

The entire trial lasted two weeks, from May 2, 2007 until May 16, 2007. The verdict was on May 16, 2007 and the sentencing on May 18, 2007. The jury was only out a couple of days.

On Thursday, May 16, 2007, I was home, alone, when I got the call that the jury was back. The verdict was in. Two days. It only took two days for the jury to come back with a verdict. My stomach, my legs, my whole being, immediately got weak. I had to be strong. Not for me, but for him; for my family. I prayed from the moment I left my house until I walked into the court room. By the time I sat down next to my oldest son, my heart was palpitating like the day he was born.

As I sat down and clued into what was being said, I could tell they were talking about Qa'id. I heard "NOT GUILTY." My heart and my mind reacted with a cry of relief. I started to cry, audibly. One second later, my oldest son leaned over and said, "Ma, they found him guilty of MURDER!" Those words hit me in a place in my soul that's reserved for a close family's death announcement. My reaction was as if I was an Academy Award winner. My tears stopped in midstream while running down my face. My whole body felt cold and numb. If my heart could have stopped, then, it would have. I don't even remember driving home that day. I often thank Allah for not letting me hear those words, Guilty of Murder!

Two days later was the sentencing. I heard what Judge College said but the only two things that stood out in my mind was the sentence of 18-Years-To- Life. His co-defendant, Mr. Lil'T got 23 to Life, because he had a weapon under disability charge. That's why they put Qa'id on trial with him. This was not Qa'id's trial. And the other thing was Judge College trying to be empathetic by saying how sorry he was and that we seemed like good parents. I could say now, it's ... *DONE ALL THE TIME*!" But That Don't Make It Right!

As we walked out of the court room, we were followed by at least two county sheriffs who followed us all the way to the courthouse entrance. My husband and oldest son were visibly upset, crying and wailing, loudly. I was so upset and angry; but I remember thinking to myself that I couldn't give them the satisfaction of showing them any emotion except rolling my eyes at them, because in my heart, I was saying, *IT AIN'T OVER.*

****

QA'ID'S PARENTS

BROTHER AND FRIEND

#1
SISTER

#2 SISTER

#3 SISTER

BROTHER

NEPHEWS

**COUSINS
ON VIDEO
CALL**

135

QA'ID

Black Mama Bear

I was again alone, driving home on automatic. I can remember singing LOUDLY and REPEATEDLY, that old spiritual hymn, *"IT'S ME, IT'S ME, IT'S ME O LORD, STANDING IN THE NEED OF PRAYER. NOT MY MOTHER, NOT MY FATHER, BUT IT'S ME O LORD, STANDING IN THE NEED OF PRAYER!* Singing it all through my "Big Duck Tears."

When I got home, I was still crying and I was just as angry as I was when he got shot the first, second and third time.

I walked around my living room coffee table for what seemed like a thousand times. As I walked, I would talk to *ALLAH* and to all of my ancestors' pictures sitting on my couch table. I begged and pleaded for help. I knew this was another test. Oh, it had become very personal because I prayed *ALLAH* to use me. The old saying, "Be careful what you pray for", is real, and I had to be up for this journey, too!

Our strength doesn't come from gold. It comes from the solid belief within our hearts.

Thinking back, I met a friend who is a priestess in the Yoruba religion. After I talked to her about my son's situation, she suggested I use one of their religious practices. I was grabbing for straws by then. This meant I had to send a donation to a priest known as Babalawo, who uses a chain and palm nuts in a process known as divination. Then, the Babalawo prescribes certain rites, offering or sacrifices – usually chickens or goats – to ensure good fortune. He sacrificed a chicken for me. I was told that the outcome of this ritual was that my son didn't do the crime, but he knew something about it. I held onto, "He didn't do the crime."

There were times when I, as that Mother Bear, would be so emotional, missing my baby son sooo much, that I would play music. The words of the songs would give me strength. I would sing to my son's soul and the songs would bring tears to my eyes. It was my own way of yearning and praying to *ALLAH*!

These were my Inspirational Songs:

Home and I Feel Good All Over by: Stephanie Mills

I'm So Into You by: Peabo Bryson

For Your Love by: Stevie Wonder

Let Me Know by: The Isley Brothers

If I Could by: Regina Belle

You Were Meant For Me by: Donny Hathaway

Through The Fire by: Chaka Khan

Win by: Amanda Cole

The Impossible Dream by: Luther Vandross

Let The Feeling Flow; I'm So Into You; and Love Like Yours And Mine by: Peabo Bryson

I'm Going Home by: Marvin Gaye (a song I found right before Qa'id was released)

JUST TO NAME A FEW THAT I LISTENED TO ALL THE TIME.

He became my life's work:

Something to do, Something to love,

and Something to look forward too!

Ten years later, I called Mr. Stewart. He did remember Qa'id's case. He didn't say much. I ask him if he could recommend another pro bono lawyer. He owned his own law firm, so I thought he would know of someone who could help us. He said if he found one he would let me know. I never heard from him again.

Our Story

The next leg of the journey was long and tedious. I would think I had a foot in the door with so many organizations who claimed to be interested in Qa'id's case. It seemed the masses believed that if he was in jail, he must be guilty, or he wouldn't be in jail. Over the years of my visiting my son in two different institutions, I can say for sure that a lot of the inmates didn't have any kind of support (a caring person nor money), so they were just stuck.

We had no money or property to pay for a lawyer or appeal.

The first lawyer we hired to appeal Qa'id's case, we paid him at least half of his $7,500 fee. When we were told the appeal was denied, we stopped paying him. He didn't do what we asked but he thought we should still pay him.

We received a lot of overdue bills. I eventually found out that he was the lawyer for Mr. Lil'T when he was in jail before this murder case. The same lawyer Mr. Lil'T called when he was asked to go and talk to the detectives right after Mr. Ahmed was shot. This lawyer knew all about Qa'id's case but never said a word. It was what this lawyer said to me that was worth more than any money we gave him. He said, very simply, "Don't give up." I put that away in my soul. I thought, why would he say that if he didn't mean it? Maybe he knows something. This lawyer's father and brothers were lawyers, and he was a former prosecutor.

After 12 years in the big house …

I had no clue that Judge Means had not been re-elected. I can remember wishing he would die. I prayed for forgiveness on that. I felt that way because he was so rude to us. I never thought he really read Qa'id's case records. He didn't even sit in on the trial, but he made all the rulings. And, when we tried to appeal Qa'id's case, he announced, "I'm not going to give him a new trial just because he's tired of being in prison." I just felt he didn't know or hadn't read anything about the case and he just didn't care because he was not the sitting judge on Qa'id's case.

There is no Mercy for those who don't show Mercy... As ALLAH is Merciful to all his Creatures.

You are the Author of your own Book of Deeds. Make sure it's worth a read on the Day of Judgment.

We create our own fate. One decision brings in another, In the End, we get to write our own Story.

You would never become you if it wasn't for your parents.

You are one out of 5 best things that ever happened to me.

"I walked on the wild side with You, Qa'id" .

****

A SHORT-STORY

ONE MAY ASK ...

*Why did you give me water? ... (Water Is
Wisdom)*

Water is ALLAH's Grace,

It's a Divine Gift,

It develops the seeds

that are planted in our hearts.

You might say: my seeds are all

rotten, I'm just an abandoned

and defeated man ...

You only lost a fortress, (a thing).

Nothing but a title,

But the most valuable prize

of a man is his heart and his soul.

Losers are those whose heart

and soul are blinded. Those

who abandoned you are the

source of cruelty.

Your heart is about to be

enlightened.

Then ... what about the suffering ...

And those tears?

The path you followed to this day

was not ALLAH's path.

You were just floating along

like a withered leaf, adrift,

with a futile cause.

Now, all this suffering means you'll

sprout and be reborn. The tears

you shed will wash away the pus

in your heart. ALLAH wouldn't

make you go through all this,

and make you shed tears, otherwise.

As the Profit (PBUH) says in the Qur'an ...

Allah knows the nature of

All men's hearts.

Then, Can a Sinner like me,

A man that has done cruel

things to man?

ALLAH says thus in the Qur'an

"my servants who have harmed

Themselves by your own excess,

God forgives all your sins.

He is truly the Most Forgiving

The Most Merciful" ... It's True

Your Job is never to succumb to

Hopelessness.

The water you drank and the

tears you shed are ALLAH'S Grace.

"Let these words soothe your Soul."

The more you cry, the more you

Feel like yourself.

In ISLAM there is no place for

hopelessness. As long as you stay

on ALLAH'S path. Commit no

atrocity and stay away from

Sin, we shall close no doors,

and you shall live as you like.

The doors of Islam are open

to everyone if they are sincere

in their wish. You will not be left

in the darkness and you will not

be chained again.

The light of enlightenment shall

wipe the darkness away from you.

A Good Scare is better than a Good Advice.

Last: "May ALLAH Grant you his Grace and,

Mercy in Abundance, and show you the

*Right Path." ****

Prison Life (The Family Is First Project)

Qa'id's spent a year in the county justice center, about 6 years in one state correctional institute and the last 6 years in another state correctional institute.

As a family we were so naïve about what life would be like behind bars. A few months after Qa'id had been locked-up, our third daughter said to me "Do we need to buy a lot of cigarettes?" Uh… It took me a minute to realize what she meant. She had been watching too many movies and too much TV. She really thought he could use cigarettes to buy favors in prison! To know her is to understand her thinking!

I would say it took Qa'id about two years of prison life to settle down and get in touch with his better self. Qa'id wanted to change how he felt about himself while he was in prison. He joined a program and asked me to join, too. At first, I didn't want to be in this group. It reminded me of one of those statistical black mamas' clubs consisting of mothers of black victims and convicted felons; but since my son asked, I gave it a try.

The Family Is First Project(TFFP) was another Godsend into our lives. It was just what we needed at that time. This project played a major role to change how we viewed each other in our family; especially between my son and his dad. The experience was priceless.

The very first time I joined the group, we women went as a group to the institution where our loved ones were housed. We had a common bond. We entered not so much as visitors, but as healers of both our hearts and the hearts of our loved ones in the program. I remember we were all treated like humans for the first time, and so were our sons. We were able to sit side-by-side, next to our sons, instead of across the table from each other. We were allowed to feel human emotions instead of trying to pretend our lives were just fine.   We talked about the real emotional struggles we were going through and have gone through. My first time speaking to the group, I can remember saying how I was not finished raising my son. I broke down because I had never spoken to him about how I felt. It was like a load lifted off of me; and yet, at the same time, I knew my son, my baby, my lust child, was not living right. I remember telling him that I wasn't done raising him. He had done things he was not proud of.

We both knew he had been blessed to still be walking around in this life.

In my eyes, ears and heart, I didn't think Qa'id was proven guilty of what he was in prison for. I think I had resolved within myself that *ALLAH* used this time to sit him down to listen so he could be guided to a better life; guided to help others; to be reminded that we come from ancestors who passed a legacy of serving others; and to give thought that his life could be much worse!

The program affected me in a way of a revelation heart opener. I thought it should be a part of the early system of correctional guidance. At first, I thought the program was just another female-driven program, a program set up just for mothers, girlfriends and sisters. I realized the program was open to not just the women of the family, but the men, too. So, I invited my husband to come to a meeting. He was probably the first and only male in attendance. Some fathers, and other family members, had not seen their loved ones in over 10 years because they did not know how to cope with the stress of having a loved one in prison. *The Family Is First Project* helped to bridge that gap.

By understanding human behavior and accepting that fact that we all will be tested in this life; but at least with an open heart, the answer will come. *Family First* is a Christian-based organization that helps guide those answers by providing a holistic approach for inmates and their loved ones, in learning how to cope with being a part of the prison system. I bought into it hook, line and sinker.

This goes to show you, when it's from GOD, GOD'S people will recognize it no matter how you address Him.

The Family Is First Project is the brainchild of Mrs. Stacie L. Johnson, Pastor and CEO.

Mrs. Johnson was blessed to write down and later form into a program what she lived through as a prison wife. She had done the last 10 years of a 20-year sentence with her husband while he was also an inmate. Her few ups and all of her downs were on full display. She became a guide for families and inmates. She eventually turned the project into a book entitled, "While You Wait." We learned that through the holistic approach of coping with being a part of the prison system was not just for the inmates but also for their loved ones. By participating and listening to each other we helped to mend the pain in our hearts that had been there for years.

Through Mrs. Johnson's guidance, Qa'id showed an interest, and with his outstanding behavior, he became one of the projects many Alumni. He also played a major role as co-facilitator of The Family Is First Project while incarcerated at the first institution he was in. And sometimes, I would be called on to give my testimony about how this positive project opened the hearts of my son, his dad, me and many other inmates and their loved ones.

Visiting my son in prison, made me so nervous, and unsure of myself ... was I dressed properly, is my top too tight, can you see my midriff, will I get beeped for wearing an under-wire bra or belt buckle. I would hold my breath going through the metal detector. Once inside the locked gates, the cost of visiting and picture taking was at least $40.00 each visit, if it was just me, if others came with me it could be a lot more. I visited at least twice a month. Most of the money was spent on food and drinks. We bought things I would never purchase on the outside.

If a guard deemed you were not dressed properly, they would suggest you buy tops or bottoms from a local Dollar Store, or you couldn't visit. No cash money or other cards were permitted inside the Institutions.

The guards at the front desk were very unfriendly, I hope they prayed every night, I know I prayed that their souls were not as cold as their jobs made them act.

My son and I would sit at a small table and pretend life was normal and we were both doing just fine, just making small talk, about family and friends. The price you pay for their mistakes. You were made to feel like a convict for the whole visit.

I can remember having a conversation with my son trying to enjoy our time together, when all of a sudden a guard was standing next to me saying, turn your legs around, as if I was inviting my son to notice something about me, to put it mildly. I was not sitting inappropriately, my legs were maybe a little to the side, trying to sit comfortably for a 4 hour visit, which is a test and a challenge. It's not like I could just get up and walk around, or go to the restroom often; the vending machines are as far as you could go. They made everybody feel like a suspect, and you were treated as though you could be breaking the law. These visits would make you want to curse. Instead you kissed the ground the guards walked on.

"I CAN IMAGINE SLAVERY BEING CLOSE TO THIS"!! You were Guilty by Association.

****

A Food Box Sample

Food Box Qa'id ordered for another inmate. Inmates would owe other inmates for various reasons, so this is a form of bartering:

(3) Georgia Peach Kool-aid

(2) Chicken Breast

(3) Carmel Corn

(1) Oreos

(2) Beef Crumbles

(10) Hot Fries (Andy's)

(10) Tunas

(10) Fish Steak and Oreo Green Chilli

(1) Nacho Cheese Doritos

(1) Cool Ranch Doritos

(1) Lays Classic Potato Chips

(2) Cinnamon Twist

(5) Cinnamon Ice Swirls

(1) Chips Ahoy Cookies

Two years later, in 2009, Qa'id was trying to better himself, so, he finally earned his GED. I was as proud of him as he was of himself. It was like he had earned a doctorate degree from a major college.

On February 06, 2015, Qa'id went on to earn his Commercial Driver's License (C.D.L.) although he couldn't take the driver's portion of the test.

At that time, he had many years left to do on his sentence, and according to prison policy, he wasn't allowed to take any college courses; but being the leader he is, Qa'id would take an interest in different subjects and would try to bring different programs or other interesting projects into the prison.

****

QA'ID'S ESSAYS

Qa'id took classes where he wrote about an array of subjects.

REFLECTION:

Writing about a time when you felt you were seeing some aspect of yourself or you actually were for the first time?

It was a Sunny Spring day in our neighborhood in a high crime area of a city where I grew up. I was 18 years old and living as if I could not be touched. Well, I would soon find out that anybody can be touched. What I mean by touched is what I do to people, it would not be done to me. I had what is called a "Big Head". So on this day which just so happened to be Easter Sunday 2006. A group of friends and I were in a Burger King Lot meeting up to go out for the day. As we were talking and getting ready to leave. I noticed a police car pulling into the parking lot slowly. I walked over to one of my friend's car to put my gun in his trunk.

When I closed the trunk of his car, I was by the sidewalk looking back at the police car, it had stopped on the side of the dumpster. (a.) Little did I know, standing right behind me on the sidewalk was a paid gunman.

He shot me in my arm first. When I felt the bullet rip through my arm, bones, blood, veins, tissue and muscles. He let off more rounds as I ran away from him. (b.) I got 20 feet away and felt a sting in my back which caused my right leg to go numb. I collapsed at that point now knowing I was hit for a second time. The nerves in my back that were connected to my leg were temporarily out of service. (c.) I knew in that moment I was just as human as the next person.

This synopsis was written for a class I was taking while I was incarcerated.

Professor's Critiques

So was the cop a set-up to get you unarmed?

Very vivid description here.

This is a powerful realization to come in this moment ... and again, I think there's more to say about the impact of the realization was for you – did it change anything afterwards? Were there more moments that illustrated it for you? Do they have more impact as we collect them over the course of a life? How long does it take for any of us to learn how very human we are?

****

"HOPE"

A letter to myself (Qa'id) ....

Dear Qa'id,

Man has your life been a real journey! In the beginning things were hard but damn did you make a cloudy day turn into a thunderstorm. It's easy to look back and judge your decisions now. Especially, after coming out on top like you did. See even though we grew up with all the teachings of the house to led us to be well off in life.

We made a choice at 13 to be "Q-Streetz." At that age music was a influence in our lives, and Lil Wayne's rap group "SQAD" was that for me. I got my name "Q. Streetz" from "T. Streetz" a rapper in the group. And the story of a new life began.

We would break the house curfew that was set by moms, by coming in the house high and hungry. I remember you would try to sneak back in the house and moms would be in the living room on the couch in the dark just waiting for the door to shut. The questions would be sliding off her tongue, "Where have you been"? "What time did I say you were supposed to be in the house"?

As I think about that, I ask myself, "What caused you at that time, in that state of mind, to start acting as if you did not care for the simple rules of the house"?

The answer, "Punishment" … Oh the word I heard so often growing up. I would miss whole summers because of my actions in school. This led me to want to be free of rules to early in life.

As I ventured off into the streets that raised me, I met kids that were doing for themselves to survive. I flicked a switch that I never turned off. I started to just hang around and watch what was going on. I eventually saw I didn't have the new things that they had bought for themselves.

The real influence was my environment and how people treated each other. Respect is earned, not given. I had little respect at first. I was my brother's ... little brother. "Yea I know you, you know karate don't you"? That's when all the fighting started. I had to show the guys I could fight and wasn't scared, just to hang around them. Once I was cool with everybody, things got real ... fast.

We would all go out to the movies just to meet up with other neighborhoods kids to fight each other. That quickly turned into shooting at each other. Even the skating rink wasn't safe to go without having to prove yourself. The culture of my community was very selfish. I say that because you really didn't care about who you hurt to come up. All things weren't bad though. I had two loving parents growing up, and still to this day I seek guidance from both of them. The things they taught me about life didn't register until I was sitting behind the walls looking at 18 to life.

"Do what is best for you"! The main thing that helped me get through it all. But, it's also the one thing that can confuse you if your mind isn't ready to face the facts of "SELF." If you didn't learn yourself, you would never have been freed from prison.

GOD had to review your intentions before he passed the word down the line to give you another chance. Stay focused on building a New Life as righteous as you can make it.

May *ALLAH* Bless you with Guidance to accomplish what is for you … and keep "Thinking For A Change". Sincerely, Qa'id

****

The Mask You Live In/ Reflection
Qa'id

It takes a lot to raise a son. It doesn't matter if we're talking about today's time or yesterday's time. The masculine influence of the world has always been in existence. This type of behavior is what you learn from adults in your life. Looking back at my own upbringing, I can see how it was embedded in my own life. As the youngest of five, I was babied a lot. Once I turned 5 years my father put me in Shu-re Ru, which is a Japanese style of Karate. And from then it was on. I could no longer cry over little things. I would take my anger out on wooden boards. My older brother would test his own skills out on me. The other kids on the block now wanted to fight me. I guess to see if I knew something they didn't, or to prove they could beat someone who could do Karate. Everything from then was physical, so with that learning experience things grew worse as I got older.

Now I was the aggressor. Going to parties to get the ladies first, then fight whoever wasn't with me and my friends. From turning a video game into a real life game (knock out king). The dominance was like a rights-of-passage. So, watching this film only bought back the memories of how I got to where I am. All my own decisions', thoughts. Because I had a lot of chances, to go a different route.

****

Health & Stress

How do you define Health and Stress?

I look at health as a system that determines how someone's life is lived. There are two forms of health, Healthy and Unhealthy. Which are the broken down forms of a person's length of life. If a person is healthy they have more of a chance to live a longer life. They have more energy to do daily activities. They have healthy organs that support energy. People who are healthy tend to be athletes.

An unhealthy person has all the opposite traits of a healthy person. They mainly are sick with some type of illness. Their organs can't fight off viruses that good. The energy of an unhealthy person is very low. This may lead to mental health problems. In which suicide is very likely. These people depend on medicine to survive. Until their health runs out and then pass away.

Stress can lead a person who is healthy to become unhealthy. If a person can't handle the stress that is given to them, they can become an unhealthy person. Stress is more of a mental state of thought. Your brain sends endorphins through the body to let it know how stressed it is.

In prison life I deal with stress by finding something positive to do. Programs usually help, but if that doesn't get the job done, I will either listen to music or workout. Self help books have given me a new outlook on life itself. So I can read books to help calm my mind.

Qa'id Salaam

****

Write about a time:

Qa'id Salaam

I realized I was in a cycle of Slavery by Another Name, when I was 2 years into my 18 to Life prison sentence. What brought me to realize this? I quickly learned that I could make choices on my own life's outcome. When I was free, I thought being in the In-Crowd was the way to success. To prove something to somebody else was the way to live. It hit me that I was the only person to have to live and deal with the consequences. When a good friend of mine told me not to fear change, just make the change better than the present. See the cycle that I was following would have brought me more misery in the end. At the time I still felt I had to prove myself worth to others, leaving my own self in a blind path to someone else's reality. I didn't want to repeat my mistakes instead I chose to learn from them. Since that point of revision, I have made a number of positive outcomes for myself. And it has landed me to be a part of other great circles to help build my foundation of a new life once I'm free from the prison I'm in. It has and will always be a mental battle to stay away from the things you've done for so long to "survive." But, knowing new ways of survival is the best thing I could have ever accomplished.

Qa'id

****

Grabbing at Straws

As a family, we had no disposable income, so we tried getting assistance from the local university and the state's Innocence Project. I also spoke to two state senators and a member of the state's House of Representatives. They all told me to let them know how things turned out. No Help! I thought, why should I vote for you?

Grabbing at straws, I wrote letters to Terry Roberts (a victim in this case) and her mother, both of whom I never got a response. As well, *Qa'id* and I wrote President Barak Obama, and I wrote the next president, Donald Trump. I even wrote a letter to Oprah (which I never mailed). I did receive a letter from President Obama the last week he was in office.

I never heard from President Trump. I never expected too!

Qa'id was told he had exhausted all his appeals.

We have indeed sent down signs that make things manifest: and ALLAH guides whom He wills to a way that is straight.

****

CHAPTER THREE

Renita's Tragedy; Meeting Mr. Phillips

I met this humble and humane man named Peter Phillips. I called him humble and humane because he did not fit the profile of most of the prosecutors I've been accustomed to seeing or hearing about, mostly in the movies and on TV. This prosecutor looked for reasonable justice.

We met when I was supporting a client during a very emotional shocking time in her life. This devastating event I found myself in made the front page of the local newspaper and the top lead story on all the local TV news channels.

I was working for a state organization helping people with developmental disabilities. My job was to assist my client, Renita C., with supervised visitations twice a week for 2 hours each day with her son, Darnell. Renita became my client in late November. This assignment lasted for 6 short weeks but turned into years of support.

Renita and I met with her son three times during the month of December. You see, her son had been removed from her home because Renita failed a drug test. She tested positive for cocaine and marijuana use.

Darnell had been placed in a foster home before his dad, Sam D., decided to have him live with him.

Renita told me that her son's father only took him in because he thought he was going to get paid like those who take care of foster children.

Sam only had custody of his son for 5 months. Renita was going to juvenile court trying to get longer visitation time with her son.

The first Thursday in December, I went to juvenile court with Renita. Sam was a no show, so, it was continued to the next week. The next scheduled court date was a week before Christmas. Court was running late, so that date got moved to after Christmas.

Renita kept saying to anybody who would listen, that Darnell's father was going to do something to her son, and she was never going to see him again. She even told the same thing to the Magistrate, but I think the Magistrate felt the same way I did: she was exaggerating. I told Renita, trying to calm her by saying, "He's not going to hurt your son." She said, "You don't know him."

I should have been thinking back to the first time I met her son and her baby's daddy. On the first scheduled visit, I took my client to pick her son up from his father. I called about 10 minutes before we arrived to get him. She lived less than 5 minutes from him.

When we got to his apartment, I got out the car and went over to meet him. He was standing in a group of maybe 3 or 4 other men. Her son was sitting on the front steps of his apartment building waiting for his mom.

I walked up to her "baby daddy", put out my hand to shake his, after I told him my name. He said very sarcastically, "How do I know if you are who you say you are? You could be anybody." He was so demeaning.

Renita had already told me he was a very mean person. I went back to my car to get my driver's license so I could show him proof of who I was. He wouldn't even look at the license. I did notice when he would say anything to my client and her son they seemed to be jumping out of their skin; they acted afraid of him. I said to myself, he had a short man's complex. He couldn't have been 5'5" tall.

Darnell was around of 2 ½ years old and was wearing a boot on his right foot, the kind of boot that's worn when you have a broken leg, foot or ankle. Daddy Sam said he broke it playing football. I thought, wow, how big were the other boys he was playing with!

I took them back to Renita's apartment. She lived with her grandmother and her oldest son, Chucky, who was around 13 years old, but very tall for his age. Darnell was so happy to be with them. They showered him with all kinds of toys.

He played, rolling on the floor, running and laughing with his big brother. Chucky noticed something was wrong with his little brother's middle finger. It was red, white and raw, like it had been burned and was healing up.

Chucky asked him, "What happen to your finger?" Without skipping a beat playing, he said, "Belisha" (Daddy Sam's girlfriend) "held my finger under some hot water." He said it like it was normal.

I tell you, his mother, his great-grandmother and his big brother couldn't stop crying. Chucky started uncontrollably saying all kinds of things like, "I'm going to kick his ass." He asked me to please take him over there so he could mess him up. Renita had a hard time trying to calm him down. I had to tell him loudly, more than once, that he couldn't go with us.

Darnell cried three different times while he was with his mom. He would say, But I don't want to go back to Daddy Sam." Renita said, But Daddy Sam loves you!" I could see this really upset his mother and his great-grandmother.

I had never seen a child react like Darnell did, after we took him home. When he got out of the car, he immediately went and sat down on the steps where he was sitting when we picked him up. He sat down, folded his hands in his lap, and dropped his head. My stomach felt queasy. I said to myself, "Oh my GOD, he is afraid."

Renita kept saying to him," Bye Darnell, mommy loves you. Bye baby." Darnell slightly waved, as if to say, ok, please go on now. My heart sunk.

Renita immediately called her case worker to report what she saw, hoping they would do something. I don't think the case worker took her very seriously because my client would call her quite often. Her case worker also called me and I told her what I witnessed; but, nothing ever came from that.

The next time we picked up Darnell, Renita bought him some new gym shoes. Darnell wore the shoes that day but, never again. Later, he told his mom that Daddy Sam sold his new shoes. After we bought the shoes, we went to the park so they could feed the ducks. Renita had brought a bag of breadcrumbs with us.

We walk to where the ducks were, and Renita handed her son the bag of bread. Soon as the ducks saw the bread being thrown on the ground, they all flew to him. It was so many, he got scared. They both ran over to me with cautious laughter. I ran to my car with them following me. We were laughing so hard, just having a good time. We all got in the car as quick as we could, still laughing hard. Then it was time for him to go back home.

The next week, when it was time for her to see her son again, we kept calling Daddy Sam but there was no answer. Renita wanted badly to see her son, so, we went to Sam's apartment. He finally came downstairs from his apartment. He said, very brashly, "Didn't I tell you, you had to pick him up from daycare."

I said, "Noooo." First of all, Renita didn't know he was in a daycare and it was the first time I had heard that, too. So, I asked, "And what daycare would that be?"

He said, with authority, "Take me over there. I'll show you." I thought to myself, "Are you asking me or telling me." I had to remember it was not about me. So, he got into my car, sat on the floor of my van, and I drove him to pick up Darnell. I was very irritated. I couldn't let him back in my car. So, I left Daddy Sam at the daycare.

All Renita wanted to do was to see Darnell for Christmas. She was not allowed because it was not on the right day of the week. Daddy Sam, again, told her if she gave him $50.00 (money she didn't have), she could see him.

It was three days after Christmas, late evening, when I got the call from Renita. She was screaming and crying incomprehensibly on the phone. She said very loudly, "I TOLD YOU THAT N...A WAS GOING TO KILL MY BABY!" Unfortunately, she was right. My special client's son, Darnell, had been murdered by his father.

Sam had punched his son Darnell in his stomach. Punched him so hard, it killed him. The police called it, "Blunt Force Trauma to the Abdomen." That's what the coroner concluded.

It took me a few minutes to completely grasp what she was saying. I had to go to her immediately. Renita was in a bad way emotionally and mentally, just a total nervous wreck. Her state of mind was all to be expected. Renita trusted no one. She was utterly paranoid.

Of course, my job description changed. I went from doing supervised visitation to somewhat of an unskilled psychiatrist. I needed to keep her calm so she could make it through her son's funeral. Then I needed to help support her while she talked to all the detectives, investigators, on through the upcoming trial in the months to come.

Renita talked with a psychiatrist, but she didn't trust her either. I'm not a psychiatrist or counselor, but, I prayed, "O' Allah, please give me the right words and a trusting heart to help guide her through this pain because she needs your help." She seemed to trust and lean on me.

Renita blamed everybody in the system, and herself, for her son's death. She blamed herself because she said if she hadn't been taking drugs in the first place, he would still be with her. She contemplated jumping out of a window several times, and she talked about other ways to ease her pain.

Not only was this traumatic for my client and her family, but I had a very hard time coping with my feelings, too. I bought a 1,000-piece jigsaw puzzle titled, *The People of Jazz* to take my mind away from the sadness and confusion of what had happened. I put it together before the trial began. This horrible experience was the leading story on the TV news and made the headlines in the newspaper for too many weeks.

It took a few months, maybe a year, for the case to be brought to trial. Finally, we were in court. While Renita son's father, Sam, was on trial, there were TV news cameras all over the courtroom and right in our faces. I sat between my client and her boyfriend, both diagnosed with Developmental Disabilities, to try to keep them calm. They both were beyond agitated, and it was very hard for both of them to be still and sit quietly. At different times I would squeeze their knees, trying to keep them calm. We had discussed this before the trial.

We made it through the trial. Of course, my client didn't understand the verdict. The Prosecutor's office had told her they were seeking the death penalty. In her mind this meant he was going to die. When that didn't happen, she was livid. She said to one of the detectives, "Ya'll said, ya'll was going to kill that 'MF'. How come he is still alive?!" He did get life without a possibility of parole, but in her mind, that was not good enough. They lied.

After the trial was over, we were standing in the courthouse hall. Mr. Phillips, the humble humane White Prosecutor I spoke about earlier, came over to me, shook my hand, and thanked me for helping my client through this hard time. I didn't know I had been noticed. I didn't help her to be noticed. She didn't trust anybody else. He made me feel proud of how I assisted my client, although, at this point, it had become a very stressful job, but somebody had to do it and I was honored to be able to help.

After the trial was over, my client wanted to sue anybody and everybody for giving her son to his father; but, to no avail. She was advised there was nothing that could be done because Sam was also her son's father and if this had happened when he was in a foster home, maybe there might be a case.

In May of 2014, while shopping at a local grocery store, I literally turned the corner and walked into Mr. Phillips. It had been a while since we had seen each other. He didn't remember my name and I didn't remember his, but that old saying, you may not know what someone may have said to you, but you can always remember how they made you feel, is so true. Without hesitating we both shook each other's hands. I don't know what came over me, I don't even remember everything I said. I just know it was all about my son, Qa'id's case.

He listened to me, and without making any promises, told me to send him what I had of Qa'id's case files and he'd take a look at it and give me his professional opinion. Every time I'd emailed him, he always emailed me back, even if he disagreed with what was said, he listened. This man was true to his word. *ANOTHER GOD- SEND!* ... So Humane!
****

Emails

November 4, 2014 at 9:04 PM

Dear Mr. Phillips,

I have been patiently waiting to hear from you. It has been six months since we spoke in the grocery store on May 4, 2014. I respect your work schedule, and I don't mean to seem impatient.

When you emailed me on July 2, 2014, you really gave me hope that at least someone was listening to me and just maybe my son could at least get a fair judgment, which you alluded to in our conversation.

If for some reason you have come to the same conclusion as I did, that there are questions in my son's trial and maybe he shouldn't be incarcerated, then we need to talk, and I can move forward. It's been 8 years this month.

Each year that he is in prison it has been devastating for him and our entire family.

I have two Affidavit(s) and other information I wish to share with you. It may help shed some light in his favor. If there is anything you can do to help resolve this injustice it would be greatly appreciated.

Thanks for all you do, Aqueelah

******

November 7, 2014 at 8:19 AM

I apologize for my tardiness in responding to you. I have looked at different things off and on since we spoke. I have reviewed a good part of the trial transcript of the case, spoken to the lead prosecutor (Ms. F. Cromwell) who no longer works in our office, and the lead detective (Mr. T. Hinkel) about what they remembered about the case and trial. I have also looked at part of the transcript and court records of (Mr. Marco T.) and the role of (Lil'T M.) in all of this. There also appeared to be someone named (Mr. Will R.) who was a witness and who may also have been involved but who I don't think was ever charged. There are a few more things I would like to review and at that time I will set up a meeting with you so we can discuss if there is anything possible that can be done.   Again, I apologize for taking so long.

Peter Phillips

******

Aqueelah ... **November 7, 2014 at 10:14 AM**

Hi Mr. Phillips,

I so appreciate your response. I look forward to talking with you soon.

I would like for you also to revisit Ms. Terry R.'s statement. She may or may not repeat what I heard her say to her mother at the trial. I do know she has since repeated it to others … and that was "I don't know him, (Qa'id). I ain't never seen him before." This is something she said when Qa'id and Mr. Lil'T M. were walking into the courtroom. I always wondered if the Public Defender or defense lawyers had just asked Ms. Terry R. if she recognized Qa'id, and she repeated that, if he would have been found Guilty of Murder. We can talk more about this statement later.

… And again, Qa'id has been contacted by the Office of the State Public Defender.

Thanks for all you do, Aqueelah *****

November 7, 2014 at 11:46 AM

Thank you for forwarding this, Aqueelah. It seems like you are making good progress with the prosecutor and I do not want to upset that. So, we will continue to review Qa'id's case, but will hold off on reaching out to Mr. Phillips for now. However, if he would like to contact me, I would be happy to speak or meet with him. And I will let you know if he does. Please keep me in the loop.

Best,

Claudia E., State Public Defender Officer

of the Public Defender Wrongful Conviction Project

******

November 8, 2014 at 12:02 PM

Thank you, Claudia E.

When I hear from Mr. Phillips, I will let you know.

Thanks for all you do,

Aqueelah

******

November 20, 2014 at 10:56 AM

Hello Aqueelah,

I have one more thing I am waiting on, which is records from DRC. Once I get them and have a chance to review them we can meet.

Peter Phillips

******

November 20, 2014 at 7:13 PM

Hi Mr. Phillips,

I'll patiently await your call.

Thank you for all you do,

Aqueelah

******

January 9, 2015 at 11:11 AM

Hi Aqueelah,

I spoke with Attorney Ural Bates about your son's situation and he agreed to look into it. You should contact him at this number..... I can't promise anything but there is a chance we might be able to do something.

******

January 9, 2015 at 11:13 AM

Hi Mr. Phillips,

THANKS FOR ALL YOU DO,

Aqueelah

******

In January 2015, Mr. Phillips suggested we hire defense lawyer, Mr. Ural Bates. Unfortunately, this lawyer was not interested in working hard. He took our money and only represented us in court, once.

When Judge Means said, "You need to bring me some new evidence. I'm not letting Qa'id out of jail just because he's tired of being in there." That was basically the last time we saw Mr. U. Bates. I don't think he thought he was going to have to work hard on this case; instead, he may have thought it was going to be easy money. He was a show man and he dressed like one, too. He got our money and stopped returning our calls after that.

******

July 2, 2015 at 10:50 AM

I haven't forgotten about you and wanted to let you know what I have done since we spoke. I reviewed the transcript you sent me at length. The prosecutor who tried the case no longer works for our office, but I was able to track her down and asked her to review the transcript and to get back with me with her thoughts about the trial. We have since spoken twice. I have also met with the lead investigator on the case – T. Hinkel- of the County Homicide Squad a couple of times about his recollections about the investigation and the trial. The only thing left for me to review is your son's statement to the police which I don't have. It is stored off site by County Police and T. Hinkel is going to get a copy of that for me. Once I review that I will have a complete picture of what went on and I can discuss my thoughts with you at that time.

I know you are anxious about this and apologize for the time it is taking. But I wanted to be thorough in order to give a fair assessment of what happened.

Sincerely,

Peter Phillips

******

December 13, 2015 at 12:18 PM

Hi, Peter Phillips,

Attorney Bates informed me that he is going to file the motion for my son this week. We pray for his success and the release of our son. … keeping you in the loop on our progress over the past year.

Thanks for all you do, Aqueelah

Hi Peter Phillips,

I hope you can answer a question for me. I'm wondering if you know what's going on with my son, Qa'id's Motion. Is it normal to take a long time to hear what the next step will be?

You know it's been 9+ years since my son has been incarcerated, and a little over a year since we retained Attorney Bates' services. With all respect to the court system and Mr. Bates, the lack of communication has become nothing less than Nerve-Racking. If this is normal, I would just like to hear that. I can't get Mr. Bates to respond to any of my messages.

I guess I'm just a little frustrated with not knowing what's next and with no communication with Attorney Bates. I really appreciate all that has been done to help in my son's case with hopes that this nightmare will end soon.

Thanks for all you do, Aqueelah

******

Feb. 18, 2016 at 8:08 AM

Hello Aqueelah,

Ural Bates has spoken to me several times about this. To my knowledge he has not actually filed a motion. Once he does he will provide a copy to me, and he and I will see whatever judge has the case and go from there.

You have to keep in mind that your son's appeals are complete and there is not a clear way for him to get what you want. Despite this, I told you and Ural Bates that if your son can convince our office and the court that he is worth giving another chance to, with serious repercussions if he screws up, we may be willing to set aside his conviction and let him plead go, something that allows him out and places him on probation for a lengthy period while he is out. So, this isn't a simple matter of filing a paper in court and getting him released.

Once Ural files his motion to set aside the conviction the case will move forward, again, to my knowledge that has not yet been done.

Peter Phillips ******

Email from me to Qa'id's Father

Feb. 18, 2016 at 9:16 AM

I just got this … it seems Ural has not totally made this clear to us, because of what Mr. Phillips is saying.

******

…To Mr. Phillips

February 18, 2016 at 9:32 AM

Thank you for getting back to me … I understand what you said.

******

March 2, 2016 at 3:44 PM

Hi Peter Phillips,

Several letters of support have been sent to
Attorney Bates on behalf of our son Qa'id.
Thanks for all you do.

Aqueelah   ******

Attorney Ural Bates …

April 23, 2016 at 7:27

Good morning. I need to reschedule our
appointment someone tried to break into my
mother's home at 2:30am so my wife and I had
to go and pick her up and we didn't get back
until around 5:30am. We are headed to her
home to secure it and get some of her things.
I'll call you after church tomorrow she is OK.

******

April 23, 2016 at 8:37 AM

Take care of your mother … I am a little anxious of course … I pray that you have some good news I will await your call tomorrow.

Thanks for all you do,

Aqueelah

******

April 23, 2016 at 2:01 PM

Thank you. She's doing good we've secured her windows and doors. I'll call you tomorrow.

******

April 25, 2016 at 10:07 AM

Can we reschedule our meeting? What's a good time for you? ******

Thanks for all you do, Aqueelah ******

April 28, 2016 at 1:10 PM

Dear Attorney Bates,

I guess your silence is to be interpreted as you haven't gotten an answer from the Judge yet. That's all we would like to hear. I was hoping for more when you ask us to meet with you. I understand that the decision for filing the motion is not in your hands. All you have to say is "I haven't heard from the judge yet" … no appointments necessary.

Aqueelah ******

May 2, 2016 at 9:45 AM

Hey Attorney Bates,

Just wondering if you think it may help if I ask Judge B. College to speak with Judge Means about my son's case. I really feel that Judge

College knows more about my son's case. Just a thought. Thanks for all you do,

Aqueelah ******

It can take years on giving you a yes or a no as to when you may or may not file the motion?

I'm just feeling very frustrated from what I feel is a lack of concern and communication.

Thanks for all you do,

Aqueelah

******

June 9, 2016 at 12:57 PM

Hey Attorney Bates,

Are you still planning to call us today?

Aqueelah ******

On March 15, 2017, I thought I would call Attorney Bates earlier than usual, so I dialed his number at 9:45 AM, to my surprise … CLICK." The phone hung up. I was pissed to say the least. I looked at my cell phone, my first instinct was to text him a few choice words. Then my phone rang. It was him calling back. … "this is Attorney Ural Bates." I was shocked. First, I thought he knew it was me, because I said my name and how obviously rude it had been to hang up like that.

He did not even let me finish saying who I was or what I wanted. It went like this:

UB: "Yes, I'm very busy, I'm on my way to court."

ME: "I understand but …" (he cuts me off)

UB: "Yes, I'll park here."

ME: "I just wanted …" (a car blows its horn)

UB: "A man is trying to hit me. I have to be in court in a few minutes. I have two trials I have to be in court for."

ME (trying to get mine in before he hangs up): "I was looking for you to call Friday."

UB:"Well, I've been very busy."

ME: I understand. When you say you are going to call, I wait all day to hear from you."

UB: Well, as I told you in court, I am only one man."

ME: I just wanted to know what you thought about the statements I sent you?"

UB: I haven't had a chance to look at it yet. I'll call you on Saturday.

ME: "That tells me something." I'm trying not to sound angry.

UB: "I got to get into court."

ME: "Ok. Bye."

We hung up.

July 24, 2016 at 10:00 AM

Dear Attorney Ural Bates &Peter Phillips,

We wanted to inform you of our intentions to also seek help from The State Public Defender Wrongful Conviction Project who has reached out to our son wanting an update of his case. Judge Means has not responded to our request, so we are seeking other assistance for Attorney Bates.

Thank you for all you do,

Aqueelah ****

Qa'id's Father

October 27, 2016 at 12:17 PM

Hi, Peter Phillips,

We are still patiently waiting to hear a reply from Judge Means about the motion that Lawyer Bates is trying to file on behalf of our son Qa'id. I'm sure if the Judge is as familiar with this case as you are … as Qa'id's parents is there anything that we can do to bring this case to the Judge's attention? Do you think it will help if we write him a letter?

******

January 23, 2017 at 2:38 PM

Dear Attorney Ural Bates

We need to ask you to talk to Mr. Sunny D. and reassure him of any concerns. He may be hesitant to call you. Thanks, Qa'id's Father

Attorney Ural Bates responds.

January 23, 2017 at 3:12 PM

Will do.

******

February 15, 2017

Hi Peter Phillips,

I've been really struggling with Judge Means' reply on my son's case. He ruled against a new trial but added that we needed to bring him something new that would lead him to change his ruling. He said he didn't want to grant a new trial just because Qa'id was tired of being incarcerated. I can understand your rationale.

I'm just not sure what we could say that would be considered new and could possibly change Judge Means' mind. Since you have read the trial transcript you can agree that the majority of the trial was speaking about his co-defendant. With NO PHYSICAL EVIDENCE on my son and the only witness being a co-defendant, I hope that Judge Means' is familiar with this case.

I don't feel that Attorney Bates has any answers. He has not spoken to us since the court date in January.

"just stuck"

Thanks for all you do, Aqueelah ******

Peter Phillips ...

February 21, 2017

Hi Aqueelah

Here is the best way I can summarize my view of your son's case. I don't think anyone viewed him as the main offender, but he was involved. Under the law of complicity, anyone who aids and abets or assists another in the commission of a crime is just as guilty as the main actor. Being guilty of complicity to a murder carries the same sentence as being guilty of murder.

The police and our prosecutors tried to get your son to cooperate against the main offender. In return for helping to convict the other person, your son would have received a plea to a lesser crime and a lesser sentence. He would have been out of jail by now. This is *done all of the time*, and as distasteful as it may be to be a "snitch", many defendants choose to do so and benefit from it. The goal of the police and our office is to always have the most serious offenders and the most involved defendant get the most time in jail. Unfortunately, in many of our serious cases it takes cooperation of lesser involved defendants like your son in order for this to work. Since most serious crimes are not committed in front of a lot of people, we often need associates of the defendant or co-defendants to make these cases. This was one of those cases.

Based on everything I have read and found from the file and talking to those involved, your son turned down the offer to get less time in return for testifying. This was against the advice of his attorney at the time. This was your son's decision. Your son went to trial and was convicted for his role in the crime. As I explained under the law complicity, he was sentenced as if he was the main offender. The sentence for murder is mandatory and not eligible for probation or early release. The case was affirmed on appeal. Legally the case was over.

There is only one legal mechanism to try at this stage of a case, since all appeals were over. A defendant can file a motion for a new trial, saying there is newly discovered evidence that was unknown or unavailable at the time he went to trial sometimes this is really the case. Other times, as here, it is the only way a defendant can have his case reconsidered by a judge. Some judges are sympathetic in a situation and to defendant like this, when even though there is no new evidence, it appears a less culpable defendant got more time than someone more involved than him in the crime.

Other judges go strictly by the law. Going strictly by the law, your son was convicted and sentenced, and his conviction and sentence were affirmed. He now regrets his decision to turn down the plea offer and testify, but that is not a legal justification to overturn his case.

This probably seems harsh but is the best way I can explain my understanding of the case. Since I did not handle it and only learned about it after it was over from you when you were a witness on the homicide I was handling, my understanding may be incomplete or inaccurate in some way. However, I think the main points are correct as I have seen similar situations many many times over the years.

I'm sorry for you and the disappointment you naturally feel at the judge's decision. Let me know if you have any other questions or if you think I have something wrong in my description of what I believe happened.

Peter Phillips

******

THE TRUTH IS, The Courts wanted Qa'id to "Snitch" on someone else in a totally different case, in turn Qa'id would be given a lesser sentence or less time in the case he was arrested for, he probably wouldn't have gotten any time, because he wouldn't have been jailed and put on trial with another person in a different case. "This is ... *DONE ALL THE TIME*", ... hence ... Apply that to both cases.

February 24, 2017

All evidence pointed to the other co-defendant and there was not any evidence whatsoever

227

against Qa'id. The court relied solely on the testimony of a co-defendant. This along with the ineffective assistance of counsel and denial of a separate trial caused him to be wrongfully convicted.

Aqueelah

******

Attorney Ural Bates,

March 11, 2017 at 10:53 AM

Hi,

We sent an email with info hoping to get a phone call from you concerning Qa'id. You said you had court to handle and would call us Thursday or Friday.

How soon can we expect to hear from you?

We are always available …Aqueelah ******

Aqueelah ...

March 23, 2017 at 10:47 PM

Hi Mr. Phillips,

As Qa'id Parents we are no longer using Attorney Bates as his lawyer. He's shown us that he doesn't have time and stated he doesn't have the resources to give to Qa'id case ... and I must say we don't have the money to pay him what he is worth. I don't think neither one of us thought it would require this much time and work.

We are not giving up we just have to seek other sources.

I will keep you informed of what path we will take.

I want you to know how much I appreciate your personal interest. If you have any ideas or guidance for us please let us know. I trust your heart.

Thanks for all you do,

Aqueelah

******

March 23, 2017 at 6:42 PM

Hi Attorney Bates,

I think it is in the best interest for our son's future to seek help from other sources. You have stated to us that you don't have the time or resources to move forward with his case. I ask that you give us all the letters of support you received and any other information you may have that may benefit his case. Please allow us to come down and pick up the information on Wednesday, March 29, 2017 at 1 PM.

THANK YOU for all your hard work and good intentions.

Aqueelah

******

Aqueelah ...

July 12, 2018 at 12:02 PM

Hi Mr. Phillips,

I just wanted to keep you informed on Qa'id's case. On June 13, 2018, a "Brief of Appellate", a reply from the Court of Appeals, was noted ... July 2, 2018. Notification of submission without argument September 17, 2018 sent to the Lead Prosecutor, Qa'id.

I pray this means it's back in the Prosecutors Office, and You will be addressing it.

Thanks for all you do, Aqueelah ******

CHAPTER FOUR

The Criminal Investigator

September 30, 2018 … Our oldest son, Qa'id's brother, called to tell me he hired Bro. Joshua O. a *Researcher/Criminal Investigator* for $500.00 to represent Qa'id. It seems Qa'id had heard about Bro. Joshua from another inmate. My oldest son wanted me to go pick up a receipt from him. When I got to his place of business, I was informed that the $500.00 was just a down payment on what was owed. He was charging us $7,500.00 to appeal Qa'id's case again. He explained that the original filing of the Sentence was incomplete from the beginning. It was like Qa'id had not been sentenced at all. He said because the Judge didn't have the court cost listed on the Sentencing Statement, the sentence was incomplete. So, we can file an appeal on that.

I called the state law library. I did my best to explain my situation to the librarian. … and without counseling me, she said the law states that it shall be included (the court cost); but it wasn't. So, the criminal investigator filed with the state for a new appeal.

On the 2nd Saturday in October 2018, we were told we needed to pay the Criminal/Researcher $7,000 more dollars. We had no idea how we could come up with that amount of money in a short time.

I decided to send this message to our family and friends to ask for their help:

Peace To Our Family and Friends:

We as the Family of Qa'id have been blessed to retain a Legal Research/Investigator to look into our son's conviction decision and records.

This Investigator has already found discrepancies in Qa'id's conviction decision.

He has assured us that he will present evidence that will show reasons to disqualify the verdict in Qa'id's case, which may lower his conviction time from 18-Life to 15 years flat. This will leave him with under 3 years left to do. As his support system we need to make a onetime payment of $7,000 dollars to the Researcher/Investigator and 2 Lawyers he works with. This payment will enable them to get Qa'id's case back in court. His parents are appealing to your heart to help us bring Qa'id home, by contributing what you can to his cause. ... Above all we still need your Prayers.

Bless you and Thank you, Qa'id's Family ... P.S. all money can be sent by, Cash App, PayPal, or through snail mail.

The money to pay the *Researcher/ Criminal Investigator* was raised and paid within four months. I was told that if he didn't get Qa'id out, we would get the money back.

Criminal Investigator Brother Joshua O.

I guess he had time to study the law. He had been incarcerated for several years. He used his talent to mostly help others who walked in his shoes: prisoners. I once said to him, if I had the money, I would send him to law school. He told me he wouldn't go because the way he does law, he can keep his foot on the lawyers' necks. He will make sure they do the right thing.

After filing with the state's Court of Appeals, Judge Means didn't want to bring Qa'id to face the courts even though there was reason. The state's Court of Appeals sent the Appeal back to the lower county Court of Appeal. That meant that the Appeal was upheld by the Higher State Court; but, Judge Means didn't want to do the right thing, so instead of bringing Qa'id back to court to let him face his new sentence in person, Judge Means just changed the sentencing on the Court Records. So, Brother Joshua filed again. This time, Brother Joshua was questioned about Qa'id using his (Brother Joshua's) address, which has nothing to do with anything. I think that was a stalling mechanism on their part. After all the work, prayers and faith, Brother Joshua couldn't believe Qa'id was getting out. He said, "See, they do whatever they want to do", meaning the Justice System. That statement reminded me of it's ... *DONE ALL THE TIME*.

Even though Brother Joshua didn't get Qa'id released, per se, I think he turned enough heads to make them think. The money we paid him was well worth it. And no, we didn't get our money back. We paid the criminal investigator, Brother Joshua, his money by the *Grace of ALLAH*. We were blessed with money from our Family and Friends. I also had a Prayer Gathering of Family and Friends … a fantastic turn out at our small home, with people showing love, encouragement and prayer all together. We had *Christians and Muslims! What a Blessed day of Joy*!

BEYOND GUILT PROGRAM

I asked a couple of friends if they knew a good advocate that worked on cases for innocent prisoners. They both gave me the same name: Attorney David Singleton. My husband and I met with him in May 2017. All of our searching to find the perfect organization was about to pay off. I read about the program and it seemed to be a perfect fit for Qa'id's situation. The perfect program with the perfect name: Beyond Guilt.

Beyond Guilt is a program that aims to do for over-punished prisoners who admit guilt what innocence projects have done for wrongfully convicted person who claim actual innocence. The mission of Beyond Guilt is to transform our punitive legal system to one focused on justice, redemption, and humanity for those over-punished.

Although Qa'id didn't want to plead guilty to anything, it was a deal that he couldn't refuse. I told him to plead guilty to whatever they say. IT'S ... *DONE ALL THE TIME.*

I contacted Mr. Singleton. He asked if we could come to his office and bring the info on Qa'id. We had a very nice first meeting. At this point I had two advocates, one paid and one in a non-profit program. I couldn't let either one of them go.

EMAILS

April 1, 2017 at 2:23 PM

To Attorney Singleton

We are in great anticipation of our meeting in regards to our son Qa'id Salaam. Please reach out to us with your schedule and we will most assuredly respond.

Respectfully,

Qa'id's Parents

******

April 10, 2017 at 10:24 AM

Good Morning Attorney Singleton

We greatly appreciate your response but we have not heard from your Secretary. We await your response/schedule for us to sit down with you.   Sincerely, Qa'id's Parents ******

Atty.. Singleton ...

April 11, 2017 at 7:06 AM

Hi, Thanks for reaching out. Please see the attached for review before we meet in May.

******

Qa'id's Father ...

August 24, 2017 at 9:19 PM

Hi Attorney Singleton ... It has been some time since we have heard anything. Is there any hopeful news or progress to share?　Thanks,

******

Atty.. Singleton ...

August 25, 2017 at 1:03 PM

Hey there. Thanks for reaching out. There are some additional things to investigate. I will be in touch soon. Qa'id's Father ... ******

November 27, 2017 at 6:44 PM

Hi, You said you would give us an update and we look forward to it coming soon. What did the co-defendant have to say? When will you go up to see our son? Qa'id's Father

******

Atty.. Singleton ...

November 27,2017 at 11:14 PM

Yep. We are overdue. I will try to set something up with Qa'id for next week and then with you there- after. Please check back at the end of week. Thanks.

******

The Darkest Hour

The darkest hour is just before Dawn … an old saying but so true!

Qa'id was beginning to get frustrated with Bro. Joshua and Attorney Singleton. How were we to know this would be the last year dealing with the court system in this way. He would say, "Man, you should let Singleton go, he ain't doing nothing," but I couldn't. I read about his program, and at that time, he had gotten maybe five or six prisoners out of prison with serious charges and they were prisoners who had been sentenced with a lot of time. And not only that, Mr. Singleton wasn't charging us a thing.

But when it came to Bro. Joshua, Qa'id seemed to have more confidence in him than in Attorney Singleton. I thought it was because he had been incarcerated, too. All my son wanted from Bro. Joshua was for him to come to see him in prison.

I held on to Hope!

I may not have wanted to be pregnant with Qa'id, but despite what my feeling were at the time, *ALLAH* knew what was best for all of us.

A Devine Movement to Teach Others About Faith!

EMAILS

Aqueelah

Attorney David Singleton ...

November 15, 2019 at 3:29 PM

(Per) - Qa'id was told that the Attorney General
called prison to get his Institutional Summary,
but the power was off in the Institution, and the
call was transferred to his Housing Unit Staff
which were the same people he talked to when
you were there. You or the Attorney General
can call and ask for the Warden's Secretary.
They're the only ones that can give it out. His
Unit Manager said he comes in Monday in the
afternoon.

******

Atty. Singleton …

November 15, 2019 at 3:29 PM

Wouldn't be Attorney General. I think
Institution is confusing attorney
general/prosecuting attorney with us. One of
my staff called to get it yesterday and is
following up. We will have it soon.

******

Aqueelah …

November 15, 2019 at 3:58 PM

Ok, thanks. I'll update Qa'id. Thanks

STEPS CLOSER TO HOMECOMING!

November 17, 2019, I wrote Attorney David Singleton a congratulatory letter for being among the 5 recipients of the Prestigious Award that Honored African American Men. … I wrote: "You are a leader with an amazing vision and have shown our Community and the American People how forgiveness and Second Chances can change those who had no future. We thank you and Pray that you are successful in getting more Incarcerated People second chances to return home. Much Success! Thank you for all you do! *Salaam/Peace.*

******

EMAILS

Atty.. Singleton wrote back

November 18, 2019

Thanks for the kind words. My goal is to have Qa'id out in time to attend next year's dinner. I will nudge the prosecutor's office later this week.

******

Aqueelah …

November 18, 2019

I'm praying it will be before then, but we'll take it, lol …

******

Atty.. Singleton reply …

November 18, 2019

Oh, Yes. Me too. I didn't mean to suggest we want a whole 'nother' year pass. I feel very positive that if things continue to go well it would be much sooner. But I can't promise anything at this point.

******

Me … Thanks

******

Aqueelah …

November 18, 2019 at 4:38 PM

Qa'id said you should receive his Institutional Records today.

******

Atty. Singleton …

November 18, 2019 at 4:43 PM

Great!

******

Aqueelah …

December 16, 2019 at 7:57PM

We know that the year is coming to an end. And since I haven't heard from you I assume nothing has been concluded in Qa'id's case. I pray that the New Year will still be young when decisions are made. We are patiently waiting. Just wanted to touch base with you. Thanks for all you do.

******

Atty. Singleton …

December 16, 2019 at 7:59 PM

I last touched base with prosecutor's office early last week and will touch base again towards end of this week. I will let you know as soon as there is something to report.

******

Aqueelah …

December 16, 2019 at 8:01 PM

Thanks

******

Atty. Singleton …

December 18, 2019 at 1:13 PM

I was able to meet again with the prosecutor today. 95 percent sure they will not oppose new trial motion with understanding that IF granted Qa'id would plead to manslaughter and get time served. I am going to draft and file motion this week and then push to get on Judge Frost's calendar as early as possible after the New Year I Jpayed this info to Qa'id and will keep you posted. ******

Aqueelah ...

December 18, 2019 at 3:07 PM

Thanks for the update.

******

I sent this information to my husband and Qa'id's #3 oldest sister ... His sister response was O.M.G.!!!!!!!!

******

Qa'id's #3 sister …

December 18, 2019 at 3:37 PM

Does that mean he can never vote in certain states?

Would he have to be on probation?

Can he live wherever he wants in or outside of the US and can he ever get that expunged?

******

Aqueelah … to my daughter

December 18, 2019 at 3:40 PM

I'll ask questions later. Let's get him home first.

******

Aqueelah … to Attorney Singleton

December 18, 2019 5:32 PM

I was so excited after reading your email. I couldn't think. Now that I have had a chance to repeat your email to others, I can properly thank you from the bottom of my heart. I will soon be able to EXHALE! … My CHILD IS COMING HOME!!!! *ALHUMDIALLAH!* … This means *All Praises Due To ALLAH!*
******

Atty. Singleton …

December 18, 2019 at 6:52 PM

Hey. Don't celebrate yet. I'm pretty confident prosecutor will support but we then have to get judge to agree. We have a good judge but at end of day it will be his call. So, no celebrating yet. Also, limit the circle of people you tell. I don't want anyone in the system finding out and then getting jealous and trying to make problems.

All of that said, continue to be positive and hopeful. Just don't get ahead of yourselves. Thx

*****

Aqueelah …

December 18, 2019 at 6:28 PM

Perfectly Understood … I just got excited. I've never been this close, but the tears are still waiting!

******

Atty. Singleton …

December 22, 2019 at 10:34 AM

I expect we will be meeting with Judge in early January. Will keep you posted.

******

Aqueelah …

December 22, 2019 at 11:26 am

Thank you for the update.******

Atty. Singleton …

December 22, 2019 at 12:46 AM

Of Course

******

Atty. Singleton …

January 6, 2020 at 10:27 AM

Good Morning. Just received word from prosecutor's office that it will officially not oppose release. This is good news I will try and get on judge's calendar for this week so the prosecutor and I can talk informally with Judge. If all goes well, then we would ask court to bring Qa'id back hopefully next week or the week after that depending on the court's availability. I feel positive and very hopeful. But we can't celebrate yet.

******

Aqueelah …

January 6, 2020 at 11:17AM

That's great news!   Patiently Waiting!

Early January 2020, I found out that Judge
Means would no longer be sitting on the bench
in our County. He was not re-elected. He was a
Republican and he was being replaced by a
Democrat, Judge Frost. I was so happy and
hopeful.

Aqueelah …

******

January 9, 2020 at 10:58 AM

Any news yet?????

******

Atty. Singleton …

January 9, 2020 at 11:30 AM

Yes. But I want to talk with Qa'id first to give him the good news and then I will give you the details. I have a request in to speak with him by phone this afternoon.

******

Aqueelah …

January. 9, 2020 at 11:34 AM

Thanks. I will wait to hear from him.

******

Atty. Singleton …

January 9, 2020 at 11:44 AM

Just to be clear, I will tell you what's up as soon as I speak to Qa'id. I know you are anxious. The news is good. Just sit tight. And if Qa'id calls you just either let him know I'm trying to call him or put me on a three way. I just want to be able to give him the news.

******

Aqueelah …

January 9, 2020 at 11:47 AM

I was talking to him when I got your message. He is waiting on your call.

******

Atty. Singleton …

January 9, 2020 at 1:04 PM

So your baby will come home on January. 27. We got his murder conviction vacated today. On 1-27 he will plead to manslaughter, get time served and be released, I'm really happy for you all.

Please do not broadcast this yet and keep it under wraps. Thanks.

******

Atty. Singleton …

January 9, 2020 at 1:08 PM

By the way. I decided just to JPay Qa'id the news. The institution was taking too long to get back to me about whether I could do a call today.

******

Aqueelah …

January 9, 2020 at 1:11 PM

All Praises Due To GOD. Thanking Him for using you, putting in your heart to do his will … Through all my Tears … Thank You

David singleton!   My test to keep it quiet.

Aqueelah …

January 9, 2020 at 1:13 PM

Qa'id said he will call me because the electric is off were he uses the Jpay. It won't be back on until 5 PM or 6 PM. ******

Atty. Singleton …

January 9, 2020 at 1:18 PM

Okay. Very important for him to keep this quiet. Don't want prisoners sabotaging him and setting him up. You're very welcome.

******

Aqueelah …

January 9, 2020 at 1:22 PM

I will give him both messages if he calls me before he gets the Jpay message. I don't want anything messing this up!!!

******

Aqueelah …

January 22, 2020 at 3:11 PM

What is the protocol for Monday morning? Do we just show up at court at 9 AM or is there something else we need to do. *"I'm so Excited."* I need to know what's next. Again*, Thank You*

******

Atty. Singleton …

January 22, 2020 at 5:21 PM

Actually, court is set for 11:00 am in Judge Frost's room (222). Qa'id will plead to manslaughter and the sentenced to time served plus post release supervision. He will not walk out of the court room with us, but will instead be taken back to the Justice Center to be processed and released. Usually that takes several hours. He should be released by the close of business on Monday and will be released from the jail. ******

Aqueelah …

January 22, 2020 at 6:19 PM

Thank you, see you on Monday

******

Aqueelah …

January 23, 2020 at 12:44 PM

Qa'id said. What are they doing about The Warrant To Convey? The Institution has to know by 12 midnight, because they won't come to get me if that's not done in time.

******

Atty. Singleton …

January 23, 2020 at 12:50 PM

I've been in touch with Qa'id about this. ''We spoke to the judge's bailiff who assured us that the order that was signed vacating the conviction and directing the sheriff to bring him is enough. We are confirming with the Institution and will get back with court as necessary.

******

Aqueelah …

January 23, 2020 at 12:56PM

I'll let him know you got this. He's just getting a little case of the nerves. That's all. *Thanks*

******

Atty. Singleton …

January 23, 2020 at 9:37 PM

They should get him tomorrow morning and bring him to the county. ******

Aqueelah …

January 23, 2020 at 9:37 PM

Thanks for letting me know   ******

Atty. Singleton …

January 25, 2020 at 5:19 PM

Hey there. If you talk with Qa'id please let him know I will be at the jail tomorrow. Thanks

******

Aqueelah …

January 25, 2020 at 8:04 PM

I did talk to him earlier. I will probably talk to him tomorrow, but I'm not sure if it will be before or after you. AGAIN, You have Changed Our Life. What a Blessing. Now please work him into your Program. ******

Atty. Singleton …

January 26, 2020 at 9:55 AM

You are very welcome.

Of course we will help him through our program.

See you tomorrow.

****

CHAPTER FIVE

BACK IN OUR CITY...

   Saturday January 25, my husband and I knew Qa'id was in town at the County Justice Center because he called us. We were so overwhelmed with excitement, we couldn't wait until Monday to see him in court, so, we tried to visit him. We were told he hadn't been assigned to a floor yet and to come back on Wednesday. It was like déjà vu all over again. Like the next day after the original arrest. I said, "By Wednesday, he'll be home,

In-sha-ALLAH, GOD Willing!"

A NEW COURT DAY...The End

January 27, 2020 at 10:25 AM we were at
the   County Courthouse (Rm. 222), Judge
Frost's court room. We were early of course.
Two of our dearest friends joined us for this
unusual trial. Bro. Joshua was in shock to the
decisions made by the court. His reactions
made me think of, *"We Do This All The Time."*

Dr. Steven Hawley was also present. He
joined us when we were trying to get a new
appeal for Qa'id. Dr. Hawley had a program
that he taught in the first prison Qa'id was in.
He was very impressed with Qa'id. The
program was called Personal Achievement
through Choices Empowering Re-entry
(P.A.C.E.R). The course was about Image,
Stock Market, Employment, Budget, Banking,
Taxes and Credit. Its main purpose was to give

a street-minded person a new way of thinking. Dr. Hawley liked Qa'id's personality and drive, he saw how Qa'id wanted to better himself. After graduating from this program, Dr. Hawley decided to ask Qa'id to become a co-facilitator in his program.

That day in court, I heard some things I knew were not in the rules of the courtroom. I wanted to say, "I Object, Your Honor!"

There was a lot of loud talking between the prosecutor, Attorney Singleton, and Judge Frost. I remember feeling somebody needs to put their hand on my knee to keep me calm. Some of the discussion was a bit unprofessional. I think the court secretary knew how it was sounding to us, so, she eventually got up and shut the door to Judge Frost's chambers. I thought to myself, "We can still hear you."

The new prosecutor on this unusual case, Prosecutor T. Ringer, sounded like he had not made up his mind as to rather Qa'id was going to stay in prison or go home, even after the original conviction and sentence had been vacated. The murder conviction was now a manslaughter charge. Qa'id had pled guilty to manslaughter. It sounded like he was still trying to show authority and let him go when *he* said so. He kept saying, "WELL WE CAN'T JUST LET HIM OUT."

This was the end of January 2020 and the beginning of COVID-19 had just been proclaimed a highly contagious virus. The prosecutor acted like Qa'id was as bad as the virus and he was out to spread it to the world.

He said Qa'id needed to get bused back to the state institution he just came from and let the bus bring him back down here, or someone could go up and pick him up tomorrow. It didn't make any sense.

He wouldn't be allowed to go back until the next day anyway because the bus had already left for its return trip. I thought we would have to wait until the next day, until he could be assigned a parole officer. All day we waited. I was going to cook something he really liked but we had no idea when he would be released.

Then around 7:40 PM, the day after his new plea, we finally got the call from his parole officer. He told us to pick Qa'id up from in front of the County Justice Center, and we needed to call him when we got there so he could bring him out. He said he would follow us home. I felt like we were doing a drive by, scoop him up and hurry up and run. I felt like somebody was going to be watching us. I sent a text message to Attorney Singleton to ask him if it was normal for the sheriff's office to follow us home. Attorney Singleton called me back and said, No. This made me have mixed feelings, like we were really breaking him out of jail. Later, after talking with Qa'id, I found out that he had requested the parole officer to follow us. He had to be nervous and paranoid. It had been a little over 13 years since he'd walked the streets of our city.

Qa'id seemed like he had just jumped into the car. This is not how I imagined nor dreamed about how this Coming Home Celebration would be.

I froze. I couldn't hug him like I wanted to. He was in the back seat, so we grabbed each other's hands and held on. I told my husband not to drive too fast because I didn't want to lose the parole officer who was following us.

Our battle was over. I wanted to cry so bad. Just like in my past, I was afraid they would follow us and take him back from us. We walked into our house, my insides were screaming, "*Thank You ALLAH*, Thank You! He made it home!"

PRAYER IS AN AMAZING EXCHANGE YOU HAND OVER YOUR WORRIES TO ALLAH AND ALLAH HANDS OVER HIS BLESSINGS TO YOU!

This BLESSING could not have been too soon because the institution he was housed in was the prison with the most inmates testing positive with the COVID-19 virus in our state.

It was said that 80% to 90% of the inmates were diagnosed with the virus.

AGAIN …To Those of you who prayed, gave money, visited him, loved him from a far, wrote a letter of support, friends who tried to help guide us, with names of advocates or just listened or asked how Qa'id was doing …

WE THANK YOU FROM THE BOTTOM

OF OUR ♥ *HEART'S.*

QUR"AN

Al-Hashr

(1)

Whatever is in the

Heavens and on Earth let

it declare the Praises are

Glory of ALLAH: for He is

The Exalted in Might, the Wise.

"BELIEVE"

Qur'an An-Nissa Sura (79)

*Whatever good, (O man!) happens to thee, is
from ALLAH, but whatever evil happens to
thee, is from they (own) soul. And...We have
sent thee as a messenger to (instruct) mankind.
And enough is ALLAH for a witness.*

*We have indeed sent down signs that make
things manifest: and ALLAH guides whom He
wills to a way that is straight.*

Qu'ran

Al-Ankaboot

Sura 29:62

*Allah enlarges the sustenance (which He gives)
to which ever of His servants He pleases, and
He (similarly) grants by (strict) measure, (as
He pleases): for ALLAH has full knowledge of
ALL things.*

EPILOGUE

(a sample of correspondence)

EXHALING on Facebook ... an

I never cried, but I definitely felt some type of way!!!
Big Facts!!!

Remember them lonely nights & the times mf ducked ya
phone calls. No mail. Mfs broke bad. Those times when ya
locker was f-up, couldn't make commissary. Ya only friend
was the store man. So don't ask me why I don't f with mf.
#trustyaprocess

---

excerpt.

K E

Mannn I heard you

Qaid

Gotta stay on a righteous path to success

K E

Factz got to it's been along time coming fuz

Qaid

I'm at work now getting it

K E

Me to Got Dam

M A

Yu ain't cry but yo eyes got watery a couple times

Qa'id

☺☺☺

S J

Man

B E

Store man is here

Qaid

Skrilla to-boa

Qa'id

Hell yea

H D

I remember!!

Qaid

You know how it was wit dem soups

H D

Yea man!!

B A

Man

T

Real shit buzz peace

Qa'id

212

N B

Boy felt like we weren't neva home make it out
that bitch

Qa'id

Big Facts

R S

4 sho I remember and I shedded a few. Shit was rough at times. But we helped each other stay afloat and that family support was vital

Qa'id

Man it was rough. And you right family played a big part.

P I K

Definitely OVERSTAND

G

Cant forget how happy I was seeing that 20dollars someone suprises me with .. the thought alone made me appreciate that person on a whole different level!

Qa'id

The surprise visits to

G

I swear

S

Word cuz they don't kno how DAT feel yo but
we gonna win big after going through this FAM
only the real can relate

Qa'id

You know we gone be good

S S

Inshallah we will

(a conversation between those who *know!)*

"LETTERS OF INTEREST"

(written 3-12-98)
Dear Mom,

I am sorry for lying to you. I hope you forgive
me. I know I get lazy sometimes, and don't
want to do anything. I will always love you.

Love,

Qa'id

letter in his words
(written) 5-16-98
Dear Mama,

I think I am treated differently here. Like when
I was suspended the first time in the third
grade, I was on a punishment. When my
brother was suspended he wasn't.
You said that, if somebody hits me and I get
suspended for more days, you would talk to the
principal too. Dad would just say you shouldn't
been around them. That makes me think that I
did something wrong. The reason why I got
into lying is because every time I got into a
fight with my older sister or one of them. It
seems like you would believe them, so I started
to lie and it seemed like you believed me, so I

kept on lying about some things. Sometimes I lied about stuff I don't need to like now. When I get whooped I have a short temper and people be messing with me at school and I know I will have to fight with one of them. I will try to control it. I am sorry for writing a fake note and putting your name on it.

Your son,

Qa'id

To: Mr. B. Cash, … While I was in segregation, I was in contact with my co-defendant Mr. Marco T. We were passing notes through the posters that worked on Sept. 15th2007. These are the two responses I had received from Mr. Marco. He still can't spell my name right. And they say we were friends! Yea right.

Qa'id J. Salaam

Notes from Co-defendant (Mr. Marco T.)

Kied, all the way real, wat made me start talkin
when I heard some shit Lil't said first man I
swore that nigga tried to switch it on me that's
why the prosecutor kept askin me about a tech!
Then you said some little shit. I felt like yall
niggaz was sayin fuck me! But I can write a
letter but I know wat ah really work is go for
appeal & call me to court room and I tell'm a
different story they go have to let you go my
lawyer told me that personally. Only thing im
salty at is yall tellin niggaz I told but ain't tellin
yall talk a little to. Yea yall got paper

Work on me just like I got on yall, but it's cool.
I don't give a fuck wat a nigga say cause I ain't
go let a nigga play me. Anyway I'll write a

letter if you want me to but I think you comin on appeal which they CAN'T DENY. You ah better if I go in there sayin a totally different story!

***

... Qa'id's first letter from jail.
December 14, 2006

Dear Ma/Dad

In the short time of me being in here. An the way
these inmates act. I realize I am different. It takes a while to become a giant, an that I am still fighting to become. I look back on my past and it shocks me, that, that wasn't what I wanted to become. I have made a lot of

mistakes as a cub. But now I am in the field of lions. So, I battle with my mind only thinking why me?? So I sit and think more and I see. I see me as a young boy being taught one thing, but nothing sunk in because I didn't believe it would happen to me. A movie life was what I saw. Where there were only two rules my life my way, an what ever happens it does for a reason. Only one I can say still stands with me an that's what ever happens it does for a reason. But, it's what I do to bring those "Happens" and "Reasons" to me. *ALLAH* says he will forgive those who repent to him willingly. So, I hope and pray he does for me. I know I haven't changed fully because I still have thoughts. So, I say to myself, I can no longer let those bad thoughts be my Actions. Tears come to my eyes as I end this letter. Know that there is more pain in life to come. I just want ya'll to know I am and I will fight to better myself and it's a must that I start mentally, I LOVE YALL *PEACE!!*

I didn't write this but when I read it I looked at myself and I was truly amazed at how I didn't listen to my own blessings.

******

Blocking My Blessings

With the things that I do I block my blessings, with the choices that I make there could be no questions. Life's a learning lesson an through my mistakes I suppose to grow, so why does my mistakes cause my love ones so much pain …

I block my blessing out here chasen fast money, the life I live is so serious so my life style ain't funny …

I block my blessing by the choices that I make.
I never had a real friend cause most brotha's
are fake ...
I blocked my blessing by turning my back on
the Most High, A lot of things happened wrong
 in my life and now I know why ...

                    Because I blocked my blessing !!!
Now I just have to use it to my advantage.

                              Sincerely,

                         Qa'id Jawwaad

Salaam

P.S. I don't want yal to write back/A man's
pride starts with himself. ME ******

07-11-07

Daddy,

As-Salaam-Alaikum!, (Peace Be Unto You),
Happy to hear from you pops. I guess hard
work never stops for a real man. Even at an old

age. The kids are blessed to have you as an overseer. I know you're the best to guide a person in the right path. I just didn't want to listen. Believing in my own ways got me here. You gave me strength in mind. And that is what keeps me going behind these walls. Today I saw the guy that got on the stand on me. I could have hit him if I wanted to. And believe me it took everything not to. I am going to try and leave him to Allah. I have other things more important to take care of now.

Where are ya'll going to move to? Have you looked yet? Tell my #2 big sister thanks for the money. I'll keep fighting to get out on this side. Oh yeah they put me in school.

Wa Alaikum As Salaam (Also Peace Be Unto You)

Love Qa'id ******

A LETTER FROM THE HOLE! (9-12-07)

Dear Mom,

How is everything? I'm okay. I'm in the hole right now. Nothing serious. All I got to do is days. So I'll be out on the 24th. I couldn't call back on my birthday, I guess the money ran out. I need some money up here. For when I get out the hole. Did the lawyer call yet? It's around that time to find out what's going on. Tell dad I said thanks for the card. Did you get the Family Reunion pictures developed yet? And did you give Tony and Billy visiting forms? Write back and let me know. *As Salaam Alaikum*

Love,

Qaid S.

P.S. I got the visiting forms. I have to wait till I get out the hole to give to the case manager.

******

Hey Qa'id (my baby boy),

I see you through eyes of LOVE. I feel that way about all of my children. Everybody wants to be heard, I see you, and I hear you. You are growing into a conscious young man, which lets me know, that you are going to be ALRIGHT!

I heard these words and I wanted to share them with you:

"Part of the blessing and challenge of being human is that you must discover your own *True God-Given Nature*. For only living in your own element can you thrive without anxiety. A fish cannot drown in water, a bird does not fall in the air. Discover what you love. Joy in what you do is not an added feature; it is a sign of deep health".

There is no greater gift you can give or receive than to honor your calling. It's why you were born, and how you can become most truly alive.

If you feel energy and excitement and a sense that life is happening for the first time, you are probably near your *God-Given Nature.*

Needless to say, if it's from *GOD* – It is Good.

Here are some questions you need to ask yourself:

1. Who am I?
2. What do I think of myself?

3. What are my strengths and weaknesses?

4. Who do I want to be?

5. Why am I here? (the larger picture)

6. Why am I important?

7. What is my mission?

8. What am I missing in my life? (like the time to read a book, a close friendship, dating, being with family?

9. What's my motivation for wanting to improve my life?

10. Am I afraid to make changes or of taking risks?

11. How can I build support for myself?

12. What am I doing in my life that's hurting me? (Smoking, Drinking too much, Etc.?

13. Am I happy?

I want all my children to be right with *ALLAH*. I can't do it for you, I know you know that. And I know that *ALLAH is Most Merciful, Most Compassionate and Forgiving. The All Knowing, Seer (Protector of all Things).*

I will continue to *PRAY* for all of us.

Love.

mama

07-25-07

Mama,

I'm salty somebody answered the phone
Wednesday and put a block on the phone. They
ain't even say hello. They was pushing buttons.
Checking the price of each call then put the
block on it. Man that ain't cool at all man.

Now I got to wait more days for you to get the
block off. Man I just did my best not to curse in
this letter.

Other than that I'm doing ok. Going to school
and Islamic service on Thursday and. I need
some more money up here. Tell everybody I
said wut up. And who ever put the block on the
phone tell them to go do something with they
self.

Love Always,

We would often talk about Sura (s) in *The Holy Qur'an* and *verses in The Holy Bible.* Qa'id wrote his opinions and thoughts about how he related to the story of Prophet Yusuf, how mass incarceration of black men, men of color and black women were treated in the system as opposed to how our Caucasian counterparts may not receive the same treatment. Many never believed Qa'id would walk out of prison early or walk out at all.

Moms & Pops, I see the jealously that his half brothers had for him. To me that could be friends that I had that wanted me to be on the level they were on or even lower. I also understand the advice given to him by his father. It was a warning to him that people will try to use your best values against you. I see that he was lied on by a woman and imprisoned for something didn't do. And while in prison, he was tested for his knowledge that Allah gave him. When he showed his wisdom, he was released. And giving a high rank or reward for his belief's and loyalty. With that his father was given his eye site and him along with his mother came to live in the kingdom in Egypt where Yusuf reined over. So, for me, I'm still in the phase of being in prison and being tested for my knowledge. Right now, I believe I am on the right path to be freed early because of the changing of my mind, (wisdom), and pursue a career path that will insure success for my family now and to come.

ASA,

Qa'id

******

Qa'id continued to struggle with his demons in his heart!!

As a mother, all I could do was pray for my baby boy; especially, when I would get letters like the following letter. Sometimes I would tell myself, "I'm so glad his grandparents were not here to witness this, and at the same time, I felt they are still praying hard for all my children … I know because I continue to pray for all my children and grandchildren!

******

Mother,

I am a young man in a circle of deception. As much as I try to keep positive, things come in front of me, through my time of being alive. I know that all those things will always be here. I like to show love in stressful times. It seems it is hard for others to do the same, those close and others who are not family. But I won' let myself be led away of what I have already put in my new path. I know I can lead myself to a good future. I have the strength to think about the outcome of a situation before I act on it. But sometimes I over look the outcomes because of my ego. Some things can't be left alone, I feel. I want to be a lot of things before I leave this life. I want to have a better understanding of my own beliefs.

I want to know more about life itself. I want to have a family of my own.

With someone I can trust and love sincerely. I really don't know why I'm here. I know I can do two things be evil or good.

I'm not an evil person but I have done evil things, Like I know I have done good things. I am important because I am here out of love. I have other's who care about me. I have some who look up to me, and because I have a purpose. I'm on a mission to survive. It used to be by any means.

But I see I can't do it that way because I have people who will be hurt by my actions if I choose the wrong way. I'm missing out on growth. It's hard to grow and change in a cage. It makes some bitter, but I try to keep an open mind and remember it is still life out there for me.

I miss my family more than anything. This is only causing tension, when it shouldn't be. Yea, I miss a few friends but I miss the feeling of a real relationship with. The motivation I have to make my life better is to not go through the same struggles I have already gone through. There are a few who are still here putting nothing but positive and uplifting words in my life. I see now that it's more to life than impressing the hood. It's always somebody out there who will accept you for you. I used to be naïve of change.

I can't say I was scared. Because I thought I was doing what I was supposed to do. But I found ways to get out of my old paths. And stick to trying to come home. I'm faced with negativity every day.

But some things are better off unsaid. Just like things I've done. If I show hate then those who feel the same will support me. So, I show that I have polish but yet I'm not on the bullshit.

To get support of those trying to make something change just like me. No! I'm not happy and content with the situation I'm in because I have no other choice. I will be happy

when I can be and do things to better myself
and my loved ones.

Always,   Qa'id

******

ALLAH brings the living out of the dead …
and the dead out of the living.

LETTER in the MUSLIM JOURNAL written by Qa'id

December 13, 2019.

In 2008, I had been incarcerated for a year. I was working on the server line in the kitchen. Well one day I was held on, out count, to prep the line with the evening meal. Due to my religion, Islam, I didn't want to stock nor serve to pork that was being prepared for chow.

Out of impulse, I cursed out the food coordinator. I called him all kinds of B's and H's. I told him I wouldn't serve that food. Well, I ended up in the hole for disrespect AND disobeying a direct order.

At that time, I thought I was all the way in the right. I just knew he couldn't make me serve that food. I mean, how could he just blatantly disregard the religious beliefs that Muslims don't eat or prepare pork I mean I can't be wrong, right?

I grew up not eating or preparing pork. Yea, I have to be right. How could I be doing 15 days in the hole for standing on my religious beliefs? He should know that I don't mess with pork. I mean I am a *"Born Muslim"*

I didn't come to prison and then change my religion as most do. These are most of the thoughts that ran through my head while I was in the hole. The most important thought was, I can't wait to get out of the hole, so I can tell my parents what had happened to me. I know they are going to have my back. At least I'm being a *"Good Muslim"*, Right?

So, when I got out of the hole. I called home and my mother answered. She asked why I hadn't called in two weeks. I told her what I did in the kitchen and that I spent the last two weeks in the hole.

She calmly said to me, "Well if you were such a *'Good Muslim.'*" You wouldn't be in there, period. You need to re-evaluate how you look at yourself and the world. You can't be a part time *Muslim*. You can't follow just the part of the Qur'an but ignore the parts that you want to. You still treat your life as if it's a game.

She told me to wake up because I was still asleep to what it means to be a *Muslim*.

When the call ended, I was lost. That was a conversation that went a totally different way than I had pictured, but it made sense to me what she was saying.

Before I came to prison I wasn't trying to hear nothing about religion. The streets and my guys were all I needed. That was then, now I know that who I keep around me is the influence I accept in my life.

So, I changed that immediately. And I am proud to say that was the last time I have been in the hole. I didn't want to repeat my mistakes; instead, I choose to learn from them. Since that point of revision, I have made a number of positive changes for myself that has landed me to be a part of other great circles to help build my foundation of a new life once I'm free from this prison.

It has and will always be a mental battle, to stay away from the things you've done for so long to "survive" but knowing new ways of survival is the best thing I could have ever accomplished.

After 13 years of being incarcerated, and trying to become a better *Muslim*. I have had more positive outcomes happen because. I have lots of changes to go a different route.

Wa Alaikum As Salaam

Qa'id

LETTER in the MUSLIM JOURNAL written by AQUEELAH

A LETTER TO MY SON

I was blessed to publish an article in the July 27, 2019 edition of the *Muslim Journal: LETTER TO MY SON, written May 30, 2018.*

Hey Qa'id ... *ASA (Peace Be Unto You)*

First let me *THANK ALLAH* for keeping you ALIVE and Well. Your life so far has been nothing short of a miracle, me knowing that *ALLAH* has always been in charge.

You are not the only one of my children I can say this about. *"All Praises Due To ALLAH."* But this time I want to say to you. You have been through a lot of drama and trauma. Most of it, I Thank *Allah* I didn't witness. But, as your mother, I have watched and felt all that Allah has put in my face: "My Test."

This isn't a "Poor Ole Mother Letter." It's a note of how much we have been blessed. You know better than me, how blessed you've been and you have grown from ...

(HOOD N.... to STREET N.... hence) "Q Streetz" (what they called you) to REAL N.... to GROWN MAN! ALL PRAISES TO ALLAH!

I don't mourn the death of who you were. I Love YOU, regardless! I can see and feel how much you have grown. You have said, "NO, WAKE UP," to the immature person you were and who others wanted you to be.

You've gotten past only loving yourself through the eyes of others, so you could love yourself and like who you have become, by the *Grace and Mercy of Allah.*

This could only happen through your being silent and listening to your Inner Perspective. *Allah* talks to your soul. Keeping it Real you were the problem you created. "Some people" want to watch you suffer. I like seeing you evolve, by being involved and helping others.

Being a victim is easy for some people to accept, but you are better than that. People will let you be a victim for your entire life.

You know you have so much to give and do Never live down what your name means. Looking at you and saying you are "ready" to control your own life, isn't easy for some others to accept either. Just prove them wrong.

Stay true to your nature, the natural state that makes your soul feel free and good.

Two Quotes:

"If people refuse to look at you in new light and they can only see you for what you were, only see you for the mistakes you've made, if they don't realize that you are not your mistakes, then they have to be blocked out of your life, if only mentally" … and *"Never get on the wrong side of small-minded people with authority"*!

"READ": I pray to see you more! I love you my baby boy!

Mama … *WAS (Peace Be Unto You, Also)*

******

Appendix

A LETTER TO TERRY ROBERTS
Hi Terry,

This is a mother's pray for help! I hope when you read this you can feel my heart the way I felt yours when you were very pregnant at my son's trial. I have been praying for you. I set right behind you and your mother. I heard you say to your mother when they bought my son Qa'id in the court room. "I don't know him, I ain't never seen him before", but they never asked you if you recognized him. I can still hear your words today. If his public defender had just asked you if you recognized him, I'm positive you would have said no, and they knew this. That's why those words were never mentioned, they knew what they were doing by saying it like that.

Our world would probably be different today. Please don't think that I think my child has never done wrong, because I know him, but I was not convinced that he murdered Ahmed.

My heart 'm sure you have as many mix feeling about this subject as I do. I'm only writing you because I am very desperate for my child. It's been almost 8 years since he has been incarcerated. I've been praying for something to change and he be released. I have been in shock and holding my breath for so long for something to end this nightmare.

I'm sure you would like to forget about the whole event, believe me, I understand. If we could have afforded a good lawyer, maybe he would not have been incarcerated. Only God knows. Qa'id knows he was not living on a good path. This whole thing could have been just to change and save his life, because he could be dead also. God has put him through this for a good reason.

Qa'id is using his experience in jail to help others, by being active in and heading up different programs to help other inmates … he is truly growing up.

I want you to know it takes a hell-of-a-lot of nerves to ask you to come forward to help him, but I see these kinds of miracles on news all the time. It says in all the "GOOD BOOKS" to step out on FAITH … this is way out of my comfort zone, but, I am a believer in GOD'S WORDS.

Mother to Mother and from my heart I'm asking you for your help!

Qa'id's Mother

****

To Terry's Mother,

I only know a mother's love for her children as I'm sure you can relate too. I'm not sure how I would advise my child if I were in your situation, and I pray you will never be in mine. In no way do I mean to belittle what you all have gone through, my intentions are to help my son, Qa'id to come home.

Our youth are killing each other, and acting like it's a badge of honor and part of growing up, and they don't have any thoughts of consequences until they are caught. I really commend your daughter, Terry, for giving her testimony as best as she could. I felt her heart and cried for how she was badgered so strongly by the courts. I can only envision all the pain she was going through mentally and emotionally not to mention her physical state.

You all were sparred of going through the whole trail. Thank GOD there was no need. My whole point of writing this note is because of what was not said at the trial. Nothing about my son that mattered in this case was mention. If my son's Public Defender had only asked Terry, "If she recognized Qa'id from that night Ahmed died, and Terry had responded, I'm very sure the jurist would not have found Qa'id

324

guilty. Qa'id was not allowed to have a separate trial because they knew there was no evidence to find him guilty. The whole trial was base on testimony against Lil' T. The only time Qa'id's name was mentioned was when a Co-defendant said Qa'id was with them, and he said he was giving his testimony, for a lesser sentence.

I'm asking you to support you daughter by encouraging her to come forward with what she knows that wasn't addressed to set the record straight.

Thank you for your understanding … Qa'id's Mother

****

A Letter To Oprah Winfrey

October 21, 2008

Hi Oprah,

I fell asleep Monday night with my TV on. At 1:06am I woke up to the sound of your voice. I don't remember anything before I heard your voice. My first instinct was to find the remote, to turn the TV off. But, in my sleepiness it took me a minute to find it. By then I was awake even more when I heard your topic.

The subject was about Marty Tankleff, being wrongly accused and convicted of murdering his parents, and spending 17 years in prison. I couldn't turn the TV off. I couldn't get back to sleep. I remember looking at the clock at 4:00am. My mind had gone into fast speed, backwards and forwards. The clock buzzed at 5:00am and I had one of the worst thinking headaches that I can ever remember.

I know I'm sending a lot of information, but this is where my thoughts lead me, after listening to your topic.

If you could pass these thoughts onto, "JAY THE LAWYER", (I DIDN'T GET HIS LAST NAME), I would be forever grateful. This is me "DARING TO DREAM".

My son Qa'id J. Salaam has been incarcerated for almost 2 years. He was arrested 2 months after his 19th birthday. The Monday after Thanksgiving in 2006. He was obviously set up by the System and an Informant, (we found out later), which is ... *DONE ALL THE TIME*.

He was accused of Robbery, or, Shooting at an Undercover Officer in a Public Park during broad daylight at Noon. This event made the Mid-Day News and the next day News Paper.

My husband and I were out of town in Philadelphia for his 40th High School Class Reunion. We had plans to come home the next day, after having lunch with one of his old class mates. Needless to say we could not fully enjoy each other's company, when our visit was cut short by a phone call from home.

We finally made it home. We had numerous phone calls waiting, from his friends who had been at the park with him. They said Qa'id did not do it, they even gave us the name of the person who they saw with the gun.

His bond was set at $250,000. I thought it was a joke, it would have been a stretch to come up with $700.00. We couldn't afford a lawyer, so he had to take a Public Defender. His court date for this offense was moved a few times.

At one court date his lawyer informed me that Qa'id had been implicated in a murder case. This was a totally different case (case II). The way the Public Defender explained it to me was he was a witness at a murder scene of this murder, and that there was one person who said my son was on the scene. The person was accused of 2 murders and several other unrelated gun chargers. It was said so nonchalantly that I really didn't take it that serious. In my mind I was still dealing with the 1st case.

While in jail on the 1st case, January 5, 2007 my son was indicted for 1st degree Murder, Murder, 1st degree Robbery and Carrying a Concealed Gun. His bond was set at $750,000. NO JOKE.

Mr. T. Marco, (codefendant II, turned State Witness and accuser), said he was giving his testimony to get a lesser sentence. He was the only one with a Private Attorney. He testified that my son and the other Codefendant (Mr. Lil' T.) where the ones who committed the murder. (Please read the court enclosed Court Trial Transcript).

Meanwhile Case I, (Robbery, Shooting at the Undercover Officer was still active. Even though Qa'id was not wearing the clothes that the said perpetrator had on, he had a total of .30 cents in his pocket, nor did he have a gun on him, the police bagged his hands and found no gun residue he was still arrested.

He was set up to get him in jail to pin a murder on him, in which he didn't do. There was not enough evidence to arrest him for this murder charge. He was bought in on trumped up charges, so he couldn't get out easy, and because he was already in jail, he looked even guiltier to the jurors. The Main Judge would not give him a separate trial, because the weak case against him depended on the testimony of codefendant II.

Qa'id had never been arrested before. In the murder case II, he was never put in a lineup of any kind, and they had absolutely no other physical evidence that implicated him in this murder.

His new Public Defender never put one person on the stand nor did he say anything in my son's defense to address his guilt.

In Case I, (Robbery, and shooting at the Undercover Officer) it was eventually dropped, dismissed, I guess. We never heard anything else about it.

Qa'id was convicted of Murder and sentenced to 18-life in the State Correctional Institution.

While he was being transported to a Maximum Security Prison, he was in the same area with his accuser, (Mr. Marco). Mr. Marco wrote Qa'id a note stating if Qa'id gets new trial he should call him to the stand again and he would change his testimony. My question is why would he do that?, did he lie the first time?, was he pushed or coerced into saying what he testified too, just to get a shorter sentence?

The Investigating Detective said that the only evidence they had against Qa'id was the testimony of his codefendant Mr. Marco, who was facing 150 years in prison. Mr. Marco actually got less time than Qa'id. Their codefendant with 2 murder convictions, received 15 years for both crimes. I don't blame him for saying whatever he needed to say for that.

My son is a big part of my heart, and right now my heart aches. I dream of him walking in our door. My dream has to come true.

He is my baby, my 5th heart beat.

The Public Defender seemed just as surprised as we did when the verdict was read.

Please give this transcript to the Lawyer, "Jay". Maybe he has some legal aids that would like to do some pro bono work, and we would have a better chance with the Supreme Court and Lawyers that are not in our State.

In our City, Black on Black Crime is at an all time high. I am hurting for the victim's family as well, but I don't want to stand by and watch my son become a victim because the Judicial System in our city needs to close a case.

My husband and I finally hired a private Lawyer, who we still owe money to. He appealed my son's case with very good questions. The 3 judges upheld the Court's decision. The private lawyer strongly encouraged us to appeal to the Supreme Court. He also suggested that we seek another Public Defender because we still owe him for the 1st appeal. This is where we are as of today, October 21, 2008.

Sincerely,

G. Aqueelah Salaam

****

November 6, 2016

To: President Barack Obama
   1600 Pennsylvania Ave NW
   Washington, DC 20500

For: Qa'id
    Correctional Institution

Written By: Qa'id Mother

Dear President Barack Obama,

I know that you have been a great President and have tried to help all Americans with your wisdom and fairness. I feel you will go down in history as the most conscientious President that America has ever had. You have given a number of incarcerated inmates leniency and shined a light on what has become a very dark circumstance that exist in our Country in PRESENT TIMES. I pray that this will be one of those times you can see the injustice and rectify it.

This is my son's life I'm talking about, I never in a million years thought we would be in this situation.

May I please have your assistance in freeing my son from a wrongly accused and conviction of murder. I'm sure if you can give this a little of your time it will be one of the easiest charges to change. I want my son to live as a productive man of society. You are our last HOPE.

AS I KNOW IT:

He's my son, he's been incarcerated since November 27th 2006, a few days short of 10 years. He was just 19 years old, (I hadn't finished raising him), when he was arrested for robbery and shooting at an undercover cop. This is what I was told. My first feelings were ... "Oh my god, he has lost his mind". I feel if that had been the case, My BLACK SON would not be alive today and I would not be writing you this letter.

This was a false arrest. There was no evidence to support this arrest, so this case never went to court. After January 5th 2007, while in jail on this charge he was charged and convicted of a murder solely based on the testimony of #1 codefendant.

My son to this day has no arrest record, even though he is serving a sentence of 18 to life in a Correctional Institution on a murder charge. It clearly states in the Black Law Dictionary pg. 1633 under the meaning of witness/accomplice witness; "A witness who is an accomplice in the crime that the defendant is charged with … (A co-defendant cannot be convicted solely on the testimony of an accomplice witness …)" [Cases: Criminal Law 507.C.J.S. Criminal Law 998.]

The Judge would not grant Qa'id a separate trial, so Qa'id was tried with a #2 codefendant using a Public Defender. The Prosecutor's arguments were focused on #2 codefendant. Who was found guilty and therefore so was my son through assumed association.

Qa'id and #2 codefendant had never met until the night in question. Qa'id's lawyer, Public Defender Attorney S. Stewart, only defense was, the Prosecutors had to show proof that

Qa'id was at the scene. Attorney Stewart LITTERALLY presented NO DEFENCE AT ALL.

Besides the young black man, (Ahmed B.), May God Rest his Soul, who was shot and killed, there was another victim, (Terry R.), who was also wounded the morning of July 20th, 2006

Mr. Ahned B. was said to be shooting also. He had in his possession a gun, drugs and money. So robbery was ruled out. Ms. Terry R. was shot in the arm. Ms. Terry was shown a lineup of pictures, one of the pictures was of my son's #2 codefendant Mr. Lil' T. My son Qa'id was never in any line up, and he was never once indentified by Ms. Terry nor was she ever asked if she recognized him during the trial.

The only witness that mentioned my son's name was the #1 codefendant, Mr. T. Marco, who became a witness for the state, and stated on the stand, "I am giving my testimony to get less time". Mr. Marco had also been charged and convicted in another murder case. Oh yeah,

Detective J. Phillips mentioned Qa'id's name when he included him in this shooting, by saying that <u>another prisoner in a totally different jail told him that he had heard that Qa'id was involved in this shooting, (HEAR SAY ... HEAR SAY).</u> ...

I since got an Affidavit from T. Johnson stating that he never made that statement to any Detective. I also got another got another affidavit from Mr. Sonny D. who was mentioned on the stand by Mr. Marco, #1 codefendant, which stated that he (Mr. Marco) and Mr. Sonny D. drove Qa'id home later after the shooting. Mr. Sonny D. signed and Affidavit rebuking that statement also.

This Is VERY CLEARLY a case of WRONGLY CONVICTED!

I have paid for appeals and waited on lawyers to do what they said they would do ... and Nothing Has Happened!

Now this is where we are ... 10 years later.

I was fortunate to have the ear of a County Humble Humane Prosecutor. He said he would review my son's case. That he did. He also talked twice to the Prosecutor Ms. Cromwell and the Detective J. Phillips who were instrumental to Qa'id's case.

My husband and I were told by the Humble Humane Prosecutor that "THEY NEVER BELIEVED MY SON DID IT"

YET ... 10 years later he is still in prison.

After reviewing my son's case and talking with the Prosecutor and Detective on the case, The Humble Humane Prosecutor gave me the name of a Lawyer who could possibly help my son get released from prison. In comes Attorney Ural Bates who has represented my son's case since January 16, 2015.

Attorney Bates led us to believe that it wouldn't take long and my son would be home in a couple of months. On December 18, 2015 Attorney Bates filed a motion to Judge G.

Means asking him if he could on behalf of my son file A Motion For A New Trial.

The holdup seems to be Common Pleas Court Judge G. Means, who I was told had not replied yet. It was stated to me by Attorney Bates when he asked Judge Means about the case, the judge said; "HAVE YOU HEARD FROM ME YET?"... ATTORNEY BATES REPLIED, "NO" ... then Judge Means replied, "THEN THAT'S WHAT YOU TELL YOUR CLIENT". We haven't heard anything since. That happened in April 2016.

An inmate of my sons once said to me

JUST BECAUSE YOU ARE CONVICTED, DON'T MEAN YOU DID IT".

I must mention that the original trial was supposed to take place in Judge Means's Courtroom, but due to his case load, the case was moved, the Retired Judge that was seated on the bench was the Honorable P. College. He was the assigned judge for my son's murder trial. I'm not sure if Judge Means is even familiar with this case.

THERE IS SO MUCH MORE!

This whole experience has taken away 10 years of my son's young life. As Qa'id's mother, I don't want him to spend another moment in jail away from his family.

I'm taking *a HUGE JUMP –LEAP OF FAITH*, as Steve Harvey says. I pray you will find a way to help us free my son from this day/nightmare.

THANKS YOU FOR ALL YOU HAVE DONE FOR OUR COUNTRY!

Sincerely,

Qa'id's Mother

****

November 7, 2016

To: President Barack Obama
    1600 Pennsylvania Ave. NW
    Washington, DC 20500

From: Qa'id J. Salaam
    A Correctional Institution

Mr. President,

Hello , My name is Qa'id Salaam, I am
currently incarcerated at a Correctional
Institution. I want to inform you on the life that
I have lived the 29yrs that I have been on this
earth. I grew up in a good home with both
biological parents. They not only told me the
right way to go in life, but they also put me in
life changing positions to make great career for
myself. The lifestyle I live before my
incarceration is what I say to be that of a low
self-esteem teenager or one who is unsure of
himself. I made a lot of selfish decision that
were born out of not knowing my purpose nor
my potential. I would do things without caring

about who it affected, as long as it got me sex and money. I didn't given even care about where I slept at night. A different friend's house would do. I thought that's all needed to make it day by day.

I was 19yrs old when I got locked up for felony murder. It was like yesterday when I heard the jury read its verdict of guilty of count 3. They found not guilty of counts 1,2,4 and 5. I didn't know the severity of what I was about to face. I am not guilty. To make it worse on me, I know I was in a different place when this murder took place but I could not prove it and my public defender did not try. He never asked any questions of any witnesses. I feel as though if I knew the things I know now, back then I wouldn't be in this situation. I know you've heard these things before but I want to tell you a few things in regard to my case and how things transpired.

I was never put into a photo lineup to be shown to a female surviving victim. While she was on the stand, the prosecutor never asked her a question about me. My mom said she overheard her tell her mom, " I don't know him, I ain't never seen him before". There is not physical evidence that links me to this crime, because I was not there ... Nothing at all places me at the scene, but a co-defendant. And from reading law books, I found that a person cannot be convicted solely on the testimony of an accomplice witness. (Black Law Dictionary).

Over my ten years of being in prison. I have grown to be a model for change. See I know that I will never fully grow to my full potential in here. Because grown to be a model for change. See, I know that I will never fully grow to my full potential in here. When I first got to prison I was a level 3 inmate. So they sent to a closed facility. I had to fit in before I could go out and be the person I am now. I was still trying to be what I thought needed to make it day by day. It took a few years of betrayals and broken promises to open my eyes to what I needed to do day by day to get out. When I realized the things I choose to do only kept me without control of my own life. I chose to change as much of that as possible. I joined programs that promoted positive change. Once I got all the certificates needed I became a facilitator for those same programs. The classes I spoke on were about a person's image. That was at the Institution.

Now, here in this Institution, I work at the prison's infirmary as a porter. Not only do I clean the place but I assist with going on emergencies to pick up inmates that have physical injuries by pushing a wheelchair or gurney and bring them back to the infirmary. I also took a CDL class and passed the writing but still waiting to take the driving part. I am now in training for a position as a facilitator here. I want to help people to change the way they feel about not being able to change. I hope that you will read this and not say that you've heard it all before. But, to give some thought to the facts that were presented to you about me and my case of injustice. Due to a lack of knowledge of the law at the time of trial this led me here to serve a 18 to life sentence. I would really appreciate your help. Thx. Qa'id Salaam

From the Office of President Barack Obama

THE WHITE HOUSE

WASHINGTON

January 17, 2017

Mrs. Gewndolyn Aqueelah Salaam
Cincinnati, Ohio

Dear Gewndolyn:

Thank you for writing, and for sharing your son's story. Today, our criminal justice system holds approximately 2.2 million Americans behind bars, at a cost to taxpayers of $80 billion per year. Many of these individuals are violent criminals who are off the streets thanks to hardworking police officers and prosecutors, but many others who are incarcerated are non-violent offenders whose punishments do not always fit their crimes. We have to make sure that our justice system is fair and effective and is doing what it can to make individuals, their families, and their communities stronger.

My Administration has taken concrete steps to enhance public safety while also making our system more just. The Department of Justice (DOJ) has instituted a series of reforms to make the Federal criminal justice system more fair and efficient and to place a greater focus on prosecuting the most serious cases. Through the Justice Reinvestment initiative, the DOJ is working with States to develop strategies to lower their incarceration numbers and to reinvest resources into communities and crime-prevention services.

Too often, the criminal justice system has worked to the detriment of young people, especially those in communities struggling to overcome poverty and other systemic challenges that widen opportunity gaps. By channeling resources into early childhood education and issuing discipline guidance to our schools, we are creating pathways to success instead of pipelines to prison, and through initiatives like *My Brother's Keeper*, we are taking steps to ensure that all young people can reach their full potential. These steps also include promoting reforms to the juvenile justice system and reaching youth before they're locked into a cycle from which they cannot recover.

For currently incarcerated individuals, my Administration has supported critical improvements to our prison system that target overcrowding, gang activity, and sexual assault. Additionally, at my direction, the Attorney General is putting into action comprehensive recommendations to reform the use of solitary confinement in the Federal prison system, including a ban on solitary confinement for juveniles and its use in response to low-level infractions. These reforms will hopefully serve as a model for State and local corrections systems.

We have also promoted rehabilitation programs proven to decrease the likelihood of a repeat offense, and we have expanded reintegration programs—such as those supported by the Second Chance Act—that work with government agencies and non-profit organizations to improve access to employment, education, housing, health care, and other critical services and support for the hundreds of thousands of inmates who are released annually and seeking to earn their second chance. In addition, I directed the

Office of Personnel Management to "ban the box" on most Federal job applications so we are not disqualifying people simply because of a mistake they made in their past.

Information about Presidential clemency can be found at www.Justice.gov/Pardon, and resources that can address reentry needs are available at CSGJusticeCenter.org/reentry/reentry-services-directory. If you are seeking relief for a State offense, you may wish to contact the Governor or another appropriate State authority to determine whether any relief is available under State law.

Thank you, again, for writing. Progress doesn't come easy, and it hasn't always followed a straight line. For the rest of my Presidency and long after, I will continue working to keep our communities safe and ensure our criminal justice system aligns with our highest ideals. I hope you continue to stay engaged as well.

Sincerely,

May 8, 2018

To: President Donald J. Trump

1600 Pennsylvania Ave. NW
Washington, DC 20500

From: Gwendolyn A. Salaam

I recently witnessed what I would call a miracle for Alice Marie Johnson, I just want to thank you for showing her such great compassion, in giving her another chance for living outside of prison.

I am writing to you on behalf of my son Qa'id J. Salaam who has served almost 12 years of an 18 to life sentence at an Ohio Correctional Institution. He has been convicted of murder. He was not viewed as the main offender. Qa'id had just met the main offender the night the crime occurred. It was argued that Qa'id was guilty of complicity. I realize that there are many others that are serving out long and sometimes unfair sentences, but Qa'id has been wrongly convicted.

According to the County Prosecutor, (one who was not the prosecutor on his case), as a personal favor for me, he reviewed Qa'id's case, which included the Trial Transcript, and conversations with the trial detectives and prosecutor. The trial Transcript is available if needed.

I am asking you to PLEASE have someone read the enclosed documents.

I am certain that you will see he had no defense, and he is not guilty of the crime he has been convicted of. He was only 18 when this crime occurred, and now soon to be 31. He is involved in many programs within the institution. He has mentally grown up to become a model inmate.

Qa'id and myself sent letters to former President Barak H. Obama asking for his help. Now I Am Asking You To Pardon Him. Sincerely

Gwendolyn A. Salaam ******

Living on the Outside

I know if I had gone to trial by myself I would not have been convicted and been incarcerated for over 13 years. Judge Means, the original judge assigned to my case, would not give me a separate trial, because it would have been my word against my Co-defendant, and there was no physical evidence. Therefore, I was tried with another Co-defendant. This Co-defendant was given 23 years to Life in prison, because he had prior felonies.

I always knew my Public Defender, Mr. Stewart did not represent me effectively. He did not ask any of the Subpoenaed Witnesses questions about me, because none of the witnesses for my defense showed up for court. "The Star witness and Vitim", Ms. Terry, was not questioned by my Court Appointed Lawyer.

Mr. Stewart only asked questions directed to the Police Officers and my Co-defendant who took the stand for the State against me. Even when he did cross-examine anyone, he was very brief. I felt my Public Defender was very cooperative with whatever was said by the other defense lawyers, Ms. Dee-Ann, and Mr. Donald who represented my #2 Co-defender, Mr. Lil'T.

He also didn't object to any questions when the Prosecutor, Mr. Cromwell, questioned other witnesses. He hardly said anything except, "No Question's Your Honor". He seemed to take on the position if they don't say your name and we don't say anything it will just go away. If he had represented me and asked pertinent questions, I wound not have been "Found guilty".

My Co-defendant Mr. Marco was the only so-called witness that testified against me. This should not have been allowed. He said whatever he had to say to try to save his own skin, even to the point of lying. Mr. Marco was looking at a lot of jail time, for two Life Sentence plus Gun Specs. He had been convicted in two Murder Cases. His life was in real jeopardy. He was coached very well by his paid Defense Lawyer. A story was made up, put him in the light of being innocent, and every answer ended with "Yes Sir, No Sir or Yes Ma'am or No.

My Co-defendant has been arrested on gun charges and other misdemeanors, to this day I don't have ONE ARREST on my record.

There were three defendants as of January 27th, 2020. I'm the only one who has been

Acquitted of all Charges ... so, to get out of those charges, I had to Plead Guilty to Manslaughter and they gave me time served. I didn't want to Plead Guilty to that, but my Mother said, "you Plead Guilty to killing a roach, if that will get you a life in this world, you can fight that case later."

I was sentence to 18 to life for a murder I didn't commit. Allah blessed me to have a lawyer believe in me and got me out after doing 13 years.

This type of treatment needs to stop. The prosecutor at my resentencing hearing said, "If Mr. Salaam would have cooperated in the beginning he would have never received that time, we never believed he was the shooter. Only that he was there". How ridiculous is our justice system? #Just Us.

"It's ... DONE ALL THE TIME ... But It Don't Make It Right"

*****

UPDATE:

Mr. Lil' T, Qa'id's co-defendant, was released from prison January 6, 2021.

"LOVE"

Tell the World, for what is Joy, If it goes unrecorded? … and what is Love if it is not shared?

Invisible wounds are the hardest to heal, for their closure depends upon the love of others, on patience, understanding and the tender gift of time.

May ALLAH Forgive All Our Sins

We Struggle – ALLAH Delivers

Justice Forever

Freedom Forever

I Am A Believer!

ALLAHU AKBAR … GOD IS THE GREATEST!!!

BIBLIOGRAPHY

1. AL QUR'AN, YUSUF ALI,

   TRANSLITERATION

2. SHEIK ABU BAKR IBN AL-ARABI

QA'ID and PARENTS

QA'ID and SISTER

QA'ID and SIBLINGS

1st THANKSGIVING

1st CAR

HAVING TO MUCH FUN!!!

QA'ID and POP's

QA'ID and MAMA

FIRST DAY HOME

QA'ID and COVID-19

MASK ON THE JOB

CANOEING IN MAMMOTH CAVE

SPECIAL INTERVIEW

BLESSED TO BE HOME

Made in the USA
Middletown, DE
06 August 2021